Important Instruction

Use the URL or QR code provided below to unlock all the online learning resources included with this Grade 8 to 9 summer bridge activities workbook.

URL	QR Code
Visit the URL below and place the book access code **http://www.lumoslearning.com/a/tedbooks** **Access Code: G8-9MLSLH-73851**	

Your online access will include;

- Skills practice resources for High School Math and ELA
- Grade-appropriate passages to improve reading skills
- Grade 8 vocabulary quizzes
- Access to Lumos Flashcube - An interactive tool for improve vocabulary practice
- Educational videos, worksheets, mobile apps, standards information and more

Additional Benefits of the Online Registration
Entry to Lumos Weekly Summer Competition
Entry to Lumos Short Story Competition

Lumos Learning
Developed by Expert Teachers

Lumos Summer Learning HeadStart, Grade 8 to 9: Includes Engaging Activities, Math, Reading, Vocabulary, Writing and Language Practice

Contributing Author   - Nicole Fernandez
Contributing Author   - Nancy Chang
Contributing Author   - Greg Applegate
Contributing Editor   - Erin Schollaert
Contributing Editor   - George Smith
Contributing Editor   - Nina Anderson
Executive Producer   - Mukunda Krishnaswamy
Designer and Illustrator - Harini N.

ISBN 13: 9781096631200

Printed in the United States of America

For permissions and additional information contact us

Lumos Information Services, LLC
PO Box 1575, Piscataway, NJ 08855-1575
http://www.LumosLearning.com

Email: support@lumoslearning.com
Tel: (732) 384-0146
Fax: (866) 283-6471

Lumos Learning
Developed by Expert Teachers

Table of Contents

Introduction

What is Summer Academic Learning Loss?

Studies show that if students take a standardized test at the end of the school year, and then repeat that test when they return in the fall, they will lose approximately four to six weeks of learning. In other words, they could potentially miss more questions in the fall than they would in the spring. This loss is commonly referred to as the summer slide.

When these standardized testing scores drop an average of one month it causes teachers to spend at least the first four to five weeks, on average, re-teaching critical material. In terms of math, students typically lose an average of two and a half months of skills and when reading and math losses are combined, it averages three months; it may even be lower for students in lower income homes.

And on average, the three areas students will typically lose ground in are spelling, vocabulary, and mathematics.

How can You Help Combat Summer Learning Loss?

Like anything, academics are something that requires practice and if they are not used regularly, you run the risk of losing them. Because of this, it is imperative your children work to keep their minds sharp over the summer. There are many ways to keep your children engaged over the summer and we're going to explore some of the most beneficial.

Start with School:

Your best source of information is your child's school. Have a conversation with your child's teacher. Tell them you are interested in working on some academics over the summer and ask what suggestions they might have. Be sure to ask about any areas your child may be struggling in and for a list of books to read over the summer. Also, talk to your child's counselor. They may have recommendations of local summer activities that will relate back to the schools and what your child needs to know. Finally, ask the front office staff for any information on currently existing after school programs (the counselor may also be able to provide this). Although after school programs may end shortly, the organizations running them will often have information on summer camps. Many of these are often free or at a very low cost to you and your family.

Stay Local:

Scour your local area for free or low cost activities and events. Most museums will have dollar days of some kind where you can get money off admission for going a certain day of the week, or a certain time. Zoos will often do the same thing. Take lunch to the park and eat outside, talking about the leaves, flowers, or anything else you can find there. Your child can pick one favorite thing and research it. Attend concerts or shows put on by local artists, musicians, or other vendors.

There are many, many other options available, you just have to explore and find them. The key here is to engage your children. Have them look online with you or search the local newspapers/ magazines. Allow them to plan the itinerary, or work with you on it, and when they get back, have them write a journal about the activity. Or, even better, have them write a letter or email to a family member about what they did.

Practice Daily:

Whether the choice is a family activity, experiencing the local environment, or staying academically focused the key is to keep your child engaged every day. That daily practice helps keep students' minds sharp and focused, ensuring they will be able to not only retain the knowledge they have learned, but in many cases begin to move ahead for the next year.

Summer Strategies for Students

Summer is here which brings a time of excitement, relaxation, and fun. School is the last thing on your mind, but that doesn't mean learning has to be on vacation too. In fact, learning is as just as important, and be just as fun (if not more), during the summer months than during the school year.

Did you know that during the summer:

- Students often lose an average of 2 and ½ months of math skills
- Students often lose 2 months of reading skills
- Teachers spend at least the first 4 to 5 weeks of the next school year reteaching important skills and concepts

Your brain is like a muscle, and like any muscle, it must be worked out regularly, and like this, your language arts and math skills are something that requires practice; if you do not use them regularly, you run the risk of losing them. So, it is very important you keep working through the summer. But, it doesn't always have to be 'school' type work. There are many ways to stay engaged, and we're going to spend a little time looking through them.

Read and Write as Often as Possible

Reading is one of the most important things you can do to keep your brain sharp and engaged. Here are some tips to remember about summer reading:

- Often, summer is the perfect time to find and read new books or books you have always been curious about. However, without your teacher, you may struggle with finding a book that is appropriate for your reading level. In this case, you just have to remember the five finger rule: open a book to a random page and begin reading aloud, holding up one finger for each word you cannot say or do not know. If you have more than five fingers visible, the book is probably too hard.

- Reading goes beyond books; there are so many other ways to read. Magazines are a great way to keep kids connected to learning, and they encourage so many different activities. National Geographic Kids, Ranger Rick, and American Girl are just a few examples. As silly as it may sound, you can also read the backs of cereal boxes and billboards to work on reading confidence and fluency, and learn many new things along the way! And thinking completely outside the box, you can also read when singing karaoke. Reading the words as they flash across the screen is a great way to build fluency. You can also turn the closed captioning on when a TV show is on to encourage literacy and reading fluency.

But writing is equally as important, and there are many things you can do to write over the summer:

- First, consider keeping a journal of you summer activities. You can detail the things you do, places you go, even people you meet. Be sure to include as much description as possible – sights, sounds, colors should all be included so you can easily remember and visualize the images. But the wonderful thing about a journal is that spelling and sentence structure are not as important. It's just the practice of actually writing that is where your focus should be. The other nice thing about a journal is that this informal writing is just for you; with journal writing you don't have to worry about anything, you just want to write.

- But if you want a little more depth to your journaling, and you want to share it with others, there is a fantastic opportunity for you with blogging. With parental approval, you can create a blog online where you can share your summer experiences with friends, family, or any others. The wonderful thing about blogs is that you can play with the privacy settings and choose who you want to see your blogs. You can make it private, where only the individuals who you send the link to can see it, or you can choose for it to be public where anyone can read it. Of course, if you are keeping a blog, you will have to make it a little more formal and pay attention to spelling, grammar, and sentences simply because you want to make sure your blog is pleasing to those who are reading it. Some popular places to post blogs are Blogger, Wordpress, Squarespace, and Quillpad.

Practice Math in Real Life

One way you can keep your brain sharp is by looking at that world around you and finding ways to include math. In this case, we're thinking of fun, practical ways to practice in your daily life.

- First, have some fun this summer with being in charge of some family projects. Suggest a fun project to complete with a parent or grandparent; decide on an area to plant some new bushes or maybe a small home project you can work on together. You can help design the project and maybe even research the best plants to plant or the best way to build the project. Then write the shopping list, making sure you determine the correct amount of supplies you will need. Without even realizing it, you will have used some basic math calculations and geometry to complete the project.

- You can also find math in shopping for groceries or while doing some back to school shopping. For each item that goes into the cart, estimate how much it will be and keep a running estimation of the total cost. Make it a competition before you go by estimating what your total bill will be and see who comes the closest. Or, you can even try and compete to see who can determine the correct total amount of tax that will be needed. And a final mental game to play while shopping is to determine the change you should receive when paying with cash. Not only is this a good skill to practice, it, more importantly, helps you make sure you're getting the correct change.

- You can even use everyday math if you are doing any traveling this summer and there are many fun ways to do this. Traveling requires money, and someone has to be in charge of the budget. You can volunteer to be the family accountant. Make a budget for the trip and keep all the receipts. Tally up the cost of the trip and even try to break it up by category – Food, fun, hotels, gas are just a few of the categories you can include. For those of you that might be looking for even more of a challenge, you can calculate what percentage of your budget has been spent on each category as well.

- And traveling by car gives many opportunities as well. Use the car odometer to calculate how far you have traveled. For an added challenge, you can see if you can calculate how much gas you used as well as how many gallons of gas per mile have been used.

Practice Daily:

Whether the choice is a family activity, experiencing the local environment, or staying academically focused the key is to keep your mind engaged every day. That daily practice helps keeps your brain sharp and focused, and helps ensure you will be able to not only retain the knowledge you learned last year but get a jump start on next year's success too!

How to Use This Workbook Effectively During Summer

This book offers a variety of state standards aligned resources, in both printed and online format, to help students learn during Summer months.

The activities in the book are organized by week and aligned with the 8th-grade learning standards. We encourage you to start at the beginning of Summer holidays. During each week, students can complete daily Math and English practice. There are five daily practice worksheets for each week. Students can log in to the online program once a week to complete reading, vocabulary and writing practice. Students can work on fun activity anytime during that week. Additionally, students can record their Summer activity through the online program.

Please note that online program also includes access to High School learning resources. This section of the online program could be used help students get a glimpse of what they would be learning in the next grade level.

Participate in the Weekly Competition and Win Prizes!

Tweet a picture of your Summer fun activity to participate in our exciting weekly competition. It could a picture of the sandcastle that you built on the beach or your sibling learning to ride a bicycle. Have fun and tweet your picture. Remember to include **@LumosLearning** and **#SummerLearning**.

Our editors will pick a winner each week and award $50 in Amazon Gift cards!

Take Advantage of the Online Resources

To access the online resources included with this book, parents and teachers can register with a FREE account. With each free signup, student accounts can be associated to enable online access for them.

Once the registration is complete, the login credentials for the created accounts will be sent in email to the id used during signup. Students can log in to their student accounts to get started with their summer learning. Parents can use the parent portal to keep track of student's progress.

How to register?

Step 1: Go to the URL or Use the QR code for the signup page
http://www.lumoslearning.com/a/tedbooks

Step 2: Place this book access code
Access Code: G8-9MLSLH-73851

Step 3: Fill in the basic details to complete registration

URL	QR Code
Visit the URL below and place the book access code **http://www.lumoslearning.com/a/tedbooks** **Access Code: G8-9MLSLH-73851**	

Lumos Short Story Competition 2020

**Write a Short Story
Based On Your Summer Experiences**

Get A Chance To Win $100 Cash Prize
+
1 Year Free Subscription To Lumos StepUp
+
Trophy With Certificate

How can my child participate in this competition?

Step 1

Visit www.lumoslearning.com/a/tedbooks and enter your
access code to create Lumos parent account and student account.
Access Code : G8-9MLSLH-73851

Step 2

After registration, your child can upload their summer story by logging into the
student portal and clicking on Lumos Short Story Competition 2020.
Last date for submission is August 31, 2020

How is this competition judged?

Lumos teachers will review students submissions in Sep 2020. Quality of submission would be
judged based on creativity, coherence and writing skills.
We recommend short stories that are less than 500 words.

Week 1 Summer Practice

Rational vs Irrational Numbers (8.NS.A.1)

Day 1

 Which of the following is an integer?

- Ⓐ -3
- Ⓑ $\frac{1}{4}$
- Ⓒ -12.5
- Ⓓ 0.454545...

 Which of the following statements is true?

- Ⓐ Every rational number is an integer.
- Ⓑ Every whole number is a rational number.
- Ⓒ Every irrational number is a natural number.
- Ⓓ Every rational number is a whole number.

Which of the following accurately describes the square root of 10?

- Ⓐ It is rational.
- Ⓑ It is irrational.
- Ⓒ It is an integer.
- Ⓓ It is a whole number.

Which of the following are rational numbers?

Instruction : Mark all the correct options. More than one option may be correct.

- Ⓐ $\frac{5}{7}$
- Ⓑ $\sqrt{10}$
- Ⓒ $\sqrt{25}$
- Ⓓ π

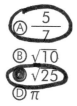

Day 1

Sympathy

I lay in sorrow, deep distressed;
My grief a proud man heard;
His looks were cold, he gave me gold,
But not a kindly word.

My sorrow passed-I paid him back
The gold he gave to me;
Then stood erect and spoke my thanks
And blessed his charity.
I lay in want, and grief, and pain;
A poor man passed my way;
He bound my head, He gave me bread,
He watched me day and night.

How shall I pay him back again
For all he did to me ?
Oh, gold is great, but greater far
Is heavenly sympathy.
-       Charles Mackay

1. The reader can tell from the third stanza that the poet is

(A) caring for a patient with a head injury.
(B) wanting company.
(C) watched and fed night and day by a poor man.
(D) greedy.

2. According to the poet, what did he feel was most important?

(A) giving away food
(B) blessing charity
(C) sympathy
(D) gold

4. What does the first stanza tell us about the poet?

- (A) The poet experienced an event which made him deeply sorrowful.
- (B) The poet wrote this poem when he was a proud man.
- (C) The poet wrote this poem when he was in need of money.
- (D) The poet was friends with the proud man.

The Lake Isle of Innisfree

I will arise and go now, and go to Innisfree,
And a small cabin build there, of clay and wattles made:
Nine bean-rows will I have there, a hive for the honey-bee;
And live alone in the bee-loud glade.

And I shall have some peace there, for peace comes dropping slow,
Dropping from the veils of the morning to where the cricket sings;
There midnight's all a glimmer, and noon a purple glow,
And evening full of the linnet's wings.

I will arise and go now, for always night and day
I hear lake water lapping with low sounds by the shore;
While I stand on the roadway, or on the pavements grey,
I hear it in the deep heart's core.

W.B. Yeats

About the poet:

William Butler Yeats was an Irish poet and a dramatist. He was one of the foremost figures of 20th-century literature and was the driving force behind the Irish literary revival. Together with Lady Gregory and Edward Martin, Yeats founded the Abbey Theatre. He served as its chief during its early years and was a pillar of the Irish literary establishment in his later years.

The well-known poem explores the poet's longing for the peace and tranquillity of Innisfree, a place where he spent a lot of time as a boy. This poem is a lyric.

Part A

According to the poem and the description, which of the following statements about the author would be true?

- Ⓐ Yeats was very famous and loved literature.
- Ⓑ Yeats was a writer and wrote a lot of poems and plays.
- Ⓒ Yeats was an Irish man and a key person in the development of Irish literature.
- Ⓓ All of the above.

Part B

Which line of the poem provides evidence that there is a cabin in Innisfree?

- Ⓐ I will arise and go now, and go to Innisfree,
- Ⓑ And a small cabin build there, of clay and wattles made:
- Ⓒ Dropping from the veils of the morning to where the cricket sings;
- Ⓓ I will arise and go now, for always night and day

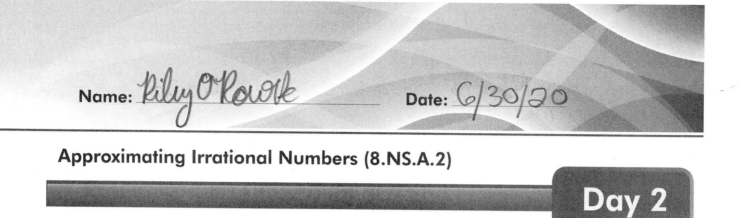
Approximating Irrational Numbers (8.NS.A.2)

Day 2

1. Between which two whole numbers does $\sqrt{5}$ lie on the number line?

   Ⓐ 1 and 2
   Ⓑ 2 and 3
   Ⓒ 3 and 4
   Ⓓ 4 and 5

2. Between which pairs of rational numbers does $\sqrt{5}$ lie on the number line?

   Ⓐ 2.0 and 2.1
   Ⓑ 2.1 and 2.2
   Ⓒ 2.2 and 2.3
   Ⓓ 2.3 and 2.4

3. Order the following numbers on a number line (least to greatest).

   Ⓐ 1.8, 1.35, 2.5, $\sqrt{5}$
   Ⓑ 1.35, $\sqrt{5}$, 1.8, 2.5
   Ⓒ 1.35, 1.8, $\sqrt{5}$, 2.5
   Ⓓ 1.35, 1.8, 2.5, $\sqrt{5}$

4. If you fill in the _____ in each of the following choices with $\sqrt{7}$, which displays the correct ordering from least to greatest?

   Ⓐ ___, 2.5, 2.63, 2.65
   Ⓑ 2.5, ___, 2.63, 2.65
   Ⓒ 2.5, 2.63, ___, 2.65
   Ⓓ 2.5, 2.63, 2.65, ___

Inferences (RL.8.1)

Day 2

The Lake Isle of Innisfree

I will arise and go now, and go to Innisfree,
And a small cabin build there, of clay and wattles made:
Nine bean-rows will I have there, a hive for the honey-bee;
And live alone in the bee-loud glade.

And I shall have some peace there, for peace comes dropping slow,
Dropping from the veils of the morning to where the cricket sings;
There midnight's all a glimmer, and noon a purple glow,
And evening full of the linnet's wings.

I will arise and go now, for always night and day
I hear lake water lapping with low sounds by the shore;
While I stand on the roadway, or on the pavements grey,
I hear it in the deep heart's core.

W.B. Yeats

About the poet:
William Butler Yeats was an Irish poet and a dramatist. He was one of the foremost figures of 20th-century literature and was the driving force behind the Irish literary revival. Together with Lady Gregory and Edward Martin, Yeats founded the Abbey Theatre. He served as its chief during its early years and was a pillar of the Irish literary establishment in his later years.

The above well-known poem explores the poet's longing for the peace and tranquility of Innisfree, a place where he spent a lot of time as a boy. This poem is a lyric.

5. After reading the poem what can you say the poet is yearning for?

   Ⓐ the lake water and the sound it makes
   Ⓑ the beehive and sound of the bees
   Ⓒ the peace and tranquility of Innisfree
   Ⓓ none of the above

6. According to the poem what do you think the age of the author is?

Ⓐ He is old and ready to retire.
Ⓑ He is a very young boy.
Ⓒ He is in his mid thirties.
Ⓓ He is a baby.

Elizabeth had done it again. She was in such a hurry; she didn't check to make sure she had everything she needed for the drive to work. Just as she slammed the door behind her, she realized, too late, that she wasn't going anywhere fast.

7. **What did Elizabeth forget?**

Ⓐ her running shoes
Ⓑ her keys
Ⓒ her briefcase
Ⓓ her workout cloths

8. **When the thunder began to roar, Mary leapt under her covers and put her hands over her ears.**

What can be inferred from Mary's reaction to the storm?

Circle the correct answer choice.

Ⓐ She enjoys thunderstorms.
Ⓑ She cannot hear well.
Ⓒ She is afraid of thunderstorms.
Ⓓ She likes to sleep.

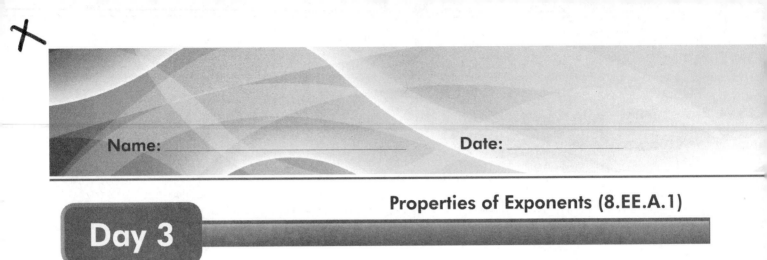

Properties of Exponents (8.EE.A.1)

Day 3

1. **Is -5² equal to (-5)² ?**

   Ⓐ Yes, because they both equal -25.
   Ⓑ Yes, because they both equal -10.
   Ⓒ Yes, because they both equal 25.
   Ⓓ No, because -5² equals -25 and (-5)² equals 25.

2. $\dfrac{X^6}{X^{-2}} =$

   Ⓐ $\dfrac{1}{X^3}$

   Ⓑ $\dfrac{1}{X^{12}}$

   Ⓒ X^4

   Ⓓ X^8

3. **Which of the following is equal to 3^{-2} ?**

   Ⓐ $\dfrac{1}{9}$

   Ⓑ -9

   Ⓒ 9

   Ⓓ $\dfrac{1}{6}$

4. **Which of the following show the proper laws of exponents?**

   Note: More than one option may be correct. Select all the correct answers.

   Ⓐ $3^2 \times 3^5 = 3^{10}$
   Ⓑ $(4^2)^3 = 4^6$

   Ⓒ $\dfrac{8^5}{8^1} = 8^4$

   Ⓓ $7^4 \times 7^4 = 7^8$

Theme (RL.8.2)

5. What is the difference between a theme and a main idea?

Ⓐ A theme is the message of a story, and the main idea is what the story is about.
Ⓑ A theme is a summary, and the main idea is a paraphrase.
Ⓒ A theme tells what the symbols mean, and the main idea is a symbol.
Ⓓ A theme is what a student writes, and a main idea is what the story is mainly about.

6. What is a universal theme?

Ⓐ a story that takes place in outer space
Ⓑ a theme that is implied
Ⓒ a common theme that could apply to anyone, anywhere, anytime
Ⓓ a theme that includes an adventure across the universe

7. The theme of a story:

Ⓐ is always a statement.
Ⓑ is usually a single word, such as "love."
Ⓒ is a question.
Ⓓ none of the above.

The Laundry

Charlie's parents always assigned him chores around the house. They would often ask him to trim the lawn, wash the dishes, and feed the dog. However, his chores never included laundry. He relied on his mother to wash his clothes for him. Charlie was an outstanding student and was recently accepted to a top college. The college he planned to attend was in New York City. Charlie was nervous about leaving Texas, where he grew up, and being so far away from his family, but he knew that the college in New York was the perfect fit for him. Before he left, his mother decided that she had better show him how to wash his own clothes because she wouldn't be there to do it for him anymore. She showed Charlie how to sort his clothes into two piles: whites and colors.

Then she showed him how much soap to use and told him when to use hot or warm water and when to use cold water. Next, she explained the different settings on the dryer and told him to be careful not to dry certain items on high heat. Charlie didn't pay much attention. He didn't see what could happen or what was so complicated about washing clothes. He planned on packing mostly t-shirts and jeans and figured that it would be hard to mess up something so simple. When Charlie arrived at school, he was completely overwhelmed with all of the exciting things to do and new people to meet. He was also careful to dedicate plenty of time to his schoolwork because he wanted to impress his professors and earn good grades. One morning Charlie woke up and found that he had no clean clothes to wear. His schedule had been so packed with activities and studying that he had managed to get through the first month of school without doing any laundry. That night, Charlie piled his soiled clothes into a large basket and headed to his dormitory's laundry room. He shoved all of his clothes into a washer, poured in the soap, and pressed the start. Half an hour later, he opened the washer and started moving the clothes into the dryer. It was then that he realized that he had skipped one very significant step. All of his white t-shirts and socks had turned pink. He had forgotten to sort his colors from his whites. Charlie had received a bright red t-shirt with his new school's logo across the front. The red dye had bled in the wash, turning all of his white clothes pink. Charlie was unhappy about his destroyed wardrobe, but he figured that there was absolutely nothing to do except to put the clothes in the dryer and hope for the best. So he transferred the clothes to a dryer and set the heat to high. After all, he was anxious to get back upstairs to his studies. An hour later, Charlie removed his clothes from the dryer and headed straight back to his dorm room. The following morning, he reached for one of his favorite t-shirts. It was slightly pink now, but he didn't have enough money to replace all of his newly pink clothes. He would have to wear them, pink or not. As he pulled the shirt over his head, he noticed that it seemed tight. He looked at himself in the mirror.

The shirt had shrunk in the dryer. It looked like he had tried to squeeze into his little sister's pink t-shirt. All Charlie could do was laugh. He called his mom and asked her to repeat her laundry instructions again.

This time, Charlie took notes.

8. What is the theme of this story? Circle the correct answer choice.

   Ⓐ Pay close attention when you are learning something new.
   Ⓑ Always ask for help.
   Ⓒ Learn how to do your laundry when you are young.
   Ⓓ Always have your parents do your laundry.

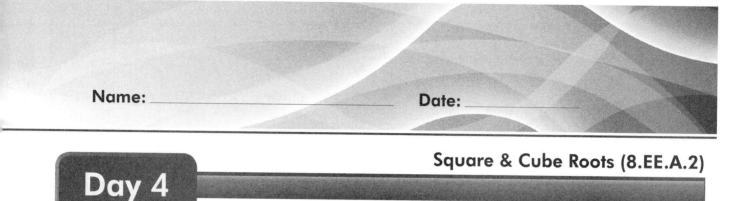

Day 4

1. **What is the cube root of 1,000?**

    Ⓐ 10

    Ⓑ 100

    Ⓒ $33\frac{1}{3}$

    Ⓓ $333\frac{1}{3}$

2. **$8\sqrt{12} \div \sqrt{15} =$**

    Ⓐ $\frac{4}{5}$

    Ⓑ $\frac{8}{5}$

    Ⓒ $\frac{16}{\sqrt{5}}$

    Ⓓ $\frac{\sqrt{5}}{8}$

3. **The square root of 75 is between which two integers?**

    Ⓐ 8 and 9
    Ⓑ 7 and 8
    Ⓒ 9 and 10
    Ⓓ 6 and 7

4. **Fill in the boxes to make the statement true**

    $\sqrt[3]{8} =$ ☐ since ☐ × ☐ × ☐ = 8

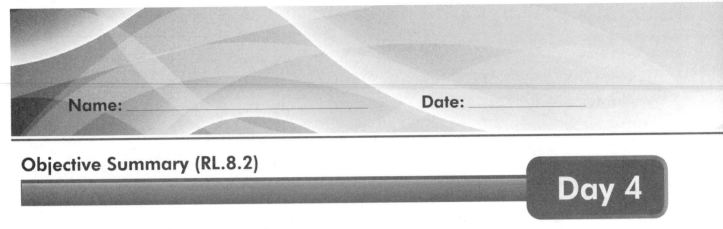
Objective Summary (RL.8.2)

Day 4

5. What is an objective summary?

Ⓐ a restatement of the main idea of a text with the addition of the writer's opinion on the idea
Ⓑ a restatement of the main idea of a text without the addition of the writer's opinion of the idea
Ⓒ a paraphrase of the text with a focus on the writer's opinion and how it affects the main idea of the passage
Ⓓ a paraphrase of the text with a focus on the reader's opinion

6. An objective summary should _____.

Ⓐ include supporting details
Ⓑ be brief, accurate, and objective
Ⓒ include both main points and supporting details
Ⓓ include the reader's opinion of the text

7. An objective summary should always _____.

Ⓐ clearly show your opinions of the text
Ⓑ clearly communicate a summary of the text
Ⓒ clearly indicate all the characters in the text
Ⓓ include at least four sentences

**The Ant and the Grasshopper
Aesop's Fable**

In a field, one summer's day, a grasshopper was hopping about, chirping and singing to its heart's content. A group of ants walked by, grunting as they struggled to carry plump kernels of corn. "Where are you going with those heavy things?" asked the grasshopper. Without stopping, the first ant replied, "To our anthill. This is the third kernel I've delivered today."

"Why not come and sing with me," teased the grasshopper, "instead of working so hard?"

"We are helping to store food for the winter," said the ant, "and think you should do the same."

"Winter is far away, and it is a glorious day to play," sang the grasshopper. But the ants went on their way and continued their hard work.

The weather soon turned cold. All the food lying in the field was covered with a thick white blanket of snow that even the grasshopper could not dig through.

Soon the grasshopper found itself dying of hunger. He staggered to the ants' hill and saw them handing out corn from the stores they had collected in the summer. He begged them for something to eat.

"What!" cried the ants in surprise, "haven't you stored anything away for the winter? What in the world were you doing all last summer?"

"I didn't have time to store any food," complained the grasshopper; "I was so busy playing music that before I knew it, the summer was gone."

The ants shook their heads in disgust, turned their backs on the grasshopper, and went on with their work.

8. What is the best summary for the story?

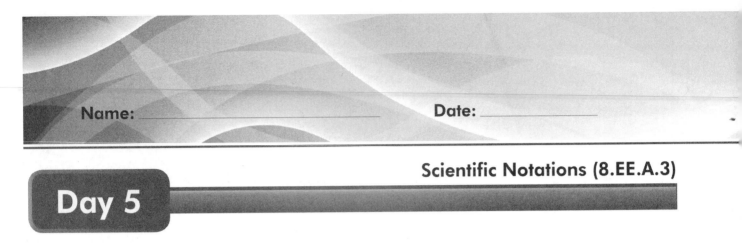
Day 5

1. In 2007, approximately 3,380,000 people visited the Statue of Liberty. Express this number in scientific notation.

   Ⓐ 0.388×10^7
   Ⓑ 3.38×10^6
   Ⓒ 33.8×10^5
   Ⓓ 338×10^4

2. The average distance from Saturn to the Sun is 890,800,000 miles. Express this number in scientific notation.

   Ⓐ 8908×10^8
   Ⓑ 8908×10^5
   Ⓒ 8.908×10^8
   Ⓓ 8.908×10^5

3. The approximate population of Los Angeles is 3.8×10^6 people. Express this number in standard notation.

   Ⓐ 380,000
   Ⓑ 3,800,000
   Ⓒ 38,000,000
   Ⓓ 380,000,000

4. Which of the following are correctly written in scientific notation?

   Note that more than one option may be correct. Select all the correct options

   Ⓐ $.032 \times 10^5$
   Ⓑ 11.002×10^{-1}
   Ⓒ 1.23×10^5
   Ⓓ 9.625×10^{-7}

Plot (RL.8.2)

Day 5

5. What are the elements of plot?

Ⓐ prelude, beginning, interlude, middle, end
Ⓑ introduction, setting, action, conflict, falling action
Ⓒ introduction, rising action, climax, falling action, resolution
Ⓓ beginning, middle, end

6. What are the two main types of conflict?

Ⓐ internal and external
Ⓑ interior and exterior
Ⓒ good and bad
Ⓓ big and little

7. What is the plot of a story?

Ⓐ the message that the author is trying to convey
Ⓑ the series of events that make up the story
Ⓒ the use of characters in a story
Ⓓ the part of a story where the characters decide what they are going to do

Walk-A-Thon

It was clear there weren't enough funds for the 8th-grade graduation ceremony at the end of the year. Big deal – why should I care? I was on the student council, but I never cared about graduation ceremonies.

It costs about $5,000.00 for the rent, equipment, the insurance, and all the other incidentals that pile up when planning a large event. Principal Dorsey told us that he didn't have the money this year. He said that if we wanted to keep the graduation tradition going, we would have to raise the money ourselves. "I'm sure we can live without the ceremony, but it would be nice to have," he told us. Then he left the meeting.

Immediately, Katrina Reynolds shot her hand in the air. She's not very popular, and I always feel kind of sorry for her. "We have to do this, you guys," Katrina gushed. "There is no way we are going to be the only class ever not to have a graduation ceremony."

Then, of course, Abbie Morelle, who was President, shot her hand in the air. I'd been on Student Council for two years, and as far as I could remember, Abbie had never let Katrina say anything without disagreeing with it. "It's very late in the year," Abbie said. "And we already have the Band Land Dance scheduled, which we don't have enough money for. We can't raise $7,000 in, like, two months."

Paulie Roman, who was treasurer, said, "According to my records, it would be more like $7,012, although we can't be certain of the precise cost of unspecified expenses related to the ceremony."

I didn't care. To me, 8th grade is pure misery, no matter what you do. If you have a great graduation ceremony at the end of it, that's like saying, "We had such a great time in all of our boring classes and with all of the bullies every day. Let's have a party to celebrate them!" But I was all for a fundraiser if it would get Abbie Morelle off Katrina's back.

I said, "Let's do a walk-a-thon. We could raise a lot of money that way."

"Walk-a-thons are stupid," Abbie said.

Paulie Roman asked, "How much money could we raise with a walk-a-thon?"

I said, "When we did a walk-a-thon for cancer research in elementary school, we raised $4,000. This school is twice as big, and people can walk farther."

"Yeah," Abbie said, "but that was for cancer. Why would anyone give us money for a graduation ceremony? Plus, someone has to organize it, and it's complicated."

That got me mad enough that I had to say, "It's not that complicated. I'll do it."

What was I thinking? I spent the next month doing almost nothing except organizing that walk-a-thon. I hate walk-a-thons, and I hate talking to people about money. I ended up doing way more than I ever wanted to.

Within the first two weeks, I could see that we weren't going to get enough. It was because we weren't raising money for something important, like cancer. So I started telling people that the money would also go for cancer research. Then, when I saw how many people were ready to give more, I just told them it was all for cancer research. I got hundreds of parents signed up, and I got businesses to donate food and decorations.

Abbie was completely jealous.

The walk-a-thon was almost a success, too. But the day before, Principal Dorsey called me into his office. He wanted to know if it was true that I had been telling people that the money would go to cancer research because he had understood the money was going or our 8th-grade graduation party. I didn't answer. He said that he was going to call some of the people who pledged money to ask them if I had said anything about cancer.

"It was the only way I could raise enough money!" I answered back, knowing the lie had caught up with me.

"Well, it was the wrong thing to do." Principal Dorsey replied. "Now, you are going to have to contact every person who donated and let them know the truth. You also may not have enough money for a graduation party now."

I knew I should never have volunteered to lead this.

8. Part A
What is the major type of conflict is in this story?

Ⓐ external: man vs fate
Ⓑ external: man vs man
Ⓒ internal: man vs himself
Ⓓ external: man vs nature

8. Part B
What is the conflict in this story?

Ⓐ there is not enough money for an 8th grade graduation party
Ⓑ who is most popular
Ⓒ who will organize the walk-a-thon
Ⓓ whether or not to have graduation

Learn Sign Language

What is American Sign Language?
American Sign Language (ASL) is a complete, complex language that employs signs made by moving the hands combined with facial expressions and postures of the body. It is the primary language of many North Americans who are deaf and is one of several communication options used by people who are deaf or hard-of-hearing.

Where did ASL originate?
The exact beginnings of ASL are not clear, but some suggest that it arose more than 200 years ago from the intermixing of local sign languages and French Sign Language (LSF, or Langue des Signes Française). Today's ASL includes some elements of LSF plus the original local sign languages, which over the years have melded and changed into a rich, complex, and mature language. Modern ASL and modern LSF are distinct languages and, while they still contain some similar signs, can no longer be understood by each other's users.

Source: https://www.nidcd.nih.gov/health/american-sign-language

Why should one learn sign language?

Enrich your cognitive skills: Sign language can enrich the cognitive development of a child. Since, different cognitive skills can be acquired as a child, learning sign language, can be implemented with practice and training in early childhood.

Make new friends: You could communicate better with the hearing-impaired people you meet, if you know the sign language, it is easier to understand and communicate effectively.

Volunteer: Use your ASL skills to interpret as a volunteer. volunteers can help in making a real difference in people's lives, with their time, effort and commitment.

Bilingual: If you are monolingual, here is an opportunity to become bilingual, with a cause.

Private chat: It would be useful to converse with a friend or in a group without anyone understanding, what you are up to.

Let's Learn the Alphabets

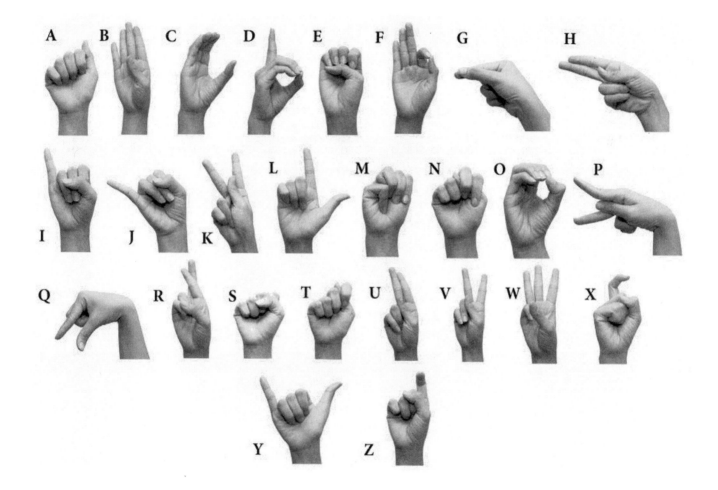

Sign language is fun if it is practiced with friends!
Partner with your friends or family members and try the following activities.

Activity

1. Communicate the following to your friend using the ASL.
   - **USA**
   - **ASL**

If your friend hasn't mastered the ASL yet, give the above alphabet chart to your friend.

2. Try saying your name in ASL using the hand gestures.

3. Have your friend communicate a funny word using ASL and you try to read it without the help of the chart. List the words you tried below.

Let's Learn the Numbers

Activity:

1. Share your postal code through ASL to your friend.
2. Communicate your home phone number in ASL to your friend.

Let's Learn Some Words

Name: _____   **Date:** _____

Week 1 Online Activity

Login to the Lumos student account and complete the following activities.

1. Reading assignment
2. Vocabulary practice
3. Write your summer diary

If you haven't created your Lumos account, use the URL and access code below to get started.

URL: http://www.lumoslearning.com/a/tedbooks

Access Code: G8-9MLSLH-73851

Week 2 Summer Practice

Solving Problems Involving Scientific Notation (8.EE.A.4)

Day 1

1. The population of California is approximately 3.7×10^7 people. The land area of California is approximately 1.6×10^5 square miles. Divide the population by the area to find the best estimate of the number of people per square mile in California.

   Ⓐ 24 people
   Ⓑ 240 people
   Ⓒ 2,400 people
   Ⓓ 24,000 people

2. Mercury is approximately 6×10^7 kilometers from the Sun. The speed of light is approximately 3×10^5 kilometers per second. Divide the distance by the speed of light to determine the approximate number of seconds it takes light to travel from the Sun to Mercury.

   Ⓐ 2 seconds
   Ⓑ 20 seconds
   Ⓒ 200 seconds
   Ⓓ 2,000 seconds

3. Simplify $(4 \times 10^6) \times (2 \times 10^3)$ and express the result in scientific notation.

   Ⓐ 8×10^9
   Ⓑ 8×10^{18}
   Ⓒ 6×10^9
   Ⓓ 6×10^{18}

4. Select the ones that correctly demonstrate the operations of scientific notation.

   Note that more than one option may be correct. Select all the correct answers.

   Ⓐ $(4.0 \times 10^3)(5.0 \times 10^5) = 2 \times 10^9$
   Ⓑ $\dfrac{4.5 \times 10^5}{9.0 \times 10^9} = 2 \times 10^4$
   Ⓒ $(2.1 \times 10^5) + (2.7 \times 10^5) = 4.8 \times 10^5$
   Ⓓ $(3.1 \times 10^5) - (2.7 \times 10^2) = 0.4 \times 10^3$

Day 1

5. During which part of a story is the setting usually introduced?

- Ⓐ introduction
- Ⓑ rising action
- Ⓒ climax
- Ⓓ resolution

6. Can there be more than one setting in a story?

- Ⓐ yes
- Ⓑ no
- Ⓒ only if the story is really long
- Ⓓ only if the story is really short

7. Which of the following can convey setting?

- Ⓐ the name of the characters
- Ⓑ the age of the characters
- Ⓒ the culture of the characters
- Ⓓ the thoughts of a character

From **Chapter 5 of Peter Pan** by J.M. Barrie

"He lay at his ease in a rough chariot drawn and propelled by his men, and instead of a right hand, he had the iron hook with which ever and anon he encouraged them to increase their pace. As dogs, this terrible man treated and addressed them, and as dogs, they obeyed him. In-person he was cadaverous [dead looking] and [dark faced], and his hair was dressed in long curls, which at a little distance looked like black candles, and gave a singularly threatening expression to his handsome countenance. His eyes were of the blue of the forget-me-not, and of a profound melancholy, save when he was plunging his hook into you, at which time two red spots appeared in them and lit them up horribly. A man of indomitable courage, it was said that the only thing he shied at was the sight of his own blood, which was thick and of an unusual color. But undoubtedly the grimmest part of him was his iron claw."

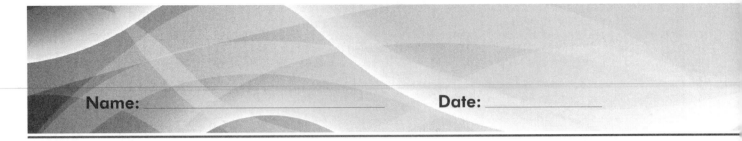
8. What is the setting of the excerpt?

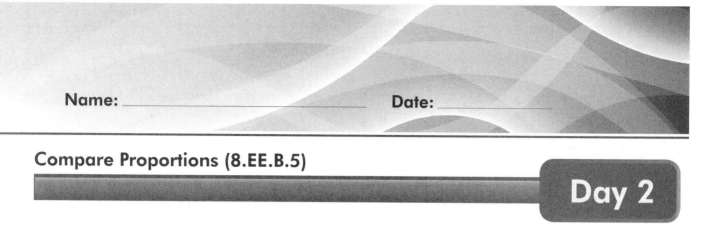

Compare Proportions (8.EE.B.5)

Day 2

1. Find the unit rate if 12 tablet cost $1,440.

   Ⓐ $100
   Ⓑ $150
   Ⓒ $120
   Ⓓ $50

2. A package of Big Bubbles Gum has 10 pieces and sells for $2.90. A package of Fruity Gum has 20 pieces and sells for $6.20. Compare the unit prices.

   Ⓐ Big Bubbles is $0.10 more per piece than Fruity.
   Ⓑ Fruity is $0.02 more per piece than Big Bubbles.
   Ⓒ They both have the same unit price.
   Ⓓ It cannot be determined.

3. The first major ski slope in Vermont has a rise of 9 feet vertically for every 54 feet horizontally. A second ski slope has a rise of 12 feet vertically for every 84 feet horizontally. Which of the following statements is true?

   Ⓐ The first slope is steeper than the second.
   Ⓑ The second slope is steeper than the first.
   Ⓒ Both slopes have the same steepness.
   Ⓓ Cannot be determined from the information given.

4. Solve for the proportion for the missing number.

   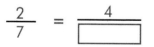

   $$\frac{2}{7} = \frac{4}{\boxed{}}$$

   Fill in the blank box with the correct answer.

Day 2

5. What is a round character?

- Ⓐ a character who has many personality traits
- Ⓑ a character who has very few personality traits
- Ⓒ a character who changes throughout the story
- Ⓓ a character who does not change throughout the story

6. Who or what is the protagonist of a story?

- Ⓐ the main character with the problem
- Ⓑ the character that is the least interesting
- Ⓒ the character that is the most interesting
- Ⓓ main character's opposing force

7. Who or what is the antagonist in a story?

- Ⓐ the main character of a story
- Ⓑ the main character's opposing force
- Ⓒ the character that is the least interesting
- Ⓓ the character that is the most interesting

Walk-A-Thon

It was clear there weren't enough funds for the 8th-grade graduation ceremony at the end of the year. Big deal – why should I care? I was on the student council, but I never cared about graduation ceremonies.

It costs about $5,000.00 for the rent, equipment, the insurance, and all the other incidentals that pile up when planning a large event. Principal Dorsey told us that he didn't have the money this year. He said that if we wanted to keep the graduation tradition going, we would have to raise the money ourselves. "I'm sure we can live without the ceremony, but it would be nice to have," he told us. Then he left the meeting.

Immediately, Katrina Reynolds shot her hand in the air. She's not very popular, and I always feel kind of sorry for her. "We have to do this, you guys," Katrina gushed. "There is no way we are going to be the only class ever not to have a graduation ceremony."

Then, of course, Abbie Morelle, who was President, shot her hand in the air. I'd been on Student Council for two years, and as far as I could remember, Abbie had never let Katrina say anything without disagreeing with it. "It's very late in the year," Abbie said. "And we already have the Band Land Dance scheduled, which we don't have enough money for. We can't raise $7,000 in, like, two months."

Paulie Roman, who was treasurer, said, "According to my records, it would be more like $7,012, although we can't be certain of the precise cost of unspecified expenses related to the ceremony."

I didn't care. To me, 8th grade is pure misery, no matter what you do. If you have a great graduation ceremony at the end of it, that's like saying, "We had such a great time in all of our boring classes and with all of the bullies every day. Let's have a party to celebrate them!" But I was all for a fundraiser if it would get Abbie Morelle off Katrina's back.

I said, "Let's do a walk-a-thon. We could raise a lot of money that way."

"Walk-a-thons are stupid," Abbie said.

Paulie Roman asked, "How much money could we raise with a walk-a-thon?"

I said, "When we did a walk-a-thon for cancer research in elementary school, we raised $4,000. This school is twice as big, and people can walk farther."

"Yeah," Abbie said, "but that was for cancer. Why would anyone give us money for a graduation ceremony? Plus, someone has to organize it, and it's complicated."

That got me mad enough that I had to say, "It's not that complicated. I'll do it."

What was I thinking? I spent the next month doing almost nothing except organizing that walk-a-thon. I hate walk-a-thons, and I hate talking to people about money. I ended up doing way more than I ever wanted to.

Within the first two weeks, I could see that we weren't going to get enough. It was because we weren't raising money for something important, like cancer. So I started telling people that the money would also go for cancer research. Then, when I saw how many people were ready to give more, I just told them it was all for cancer research. I got hundreds of parents signed up, and I got businesses to do nate food and decorations.

Abbie was completely jealous.

The walk-a-thon was almost a success, too. But the day before, Principal Dorsey called me into his office. He wanted to know if it was true that I had been telling people that the money would go to cancer research because he had understood the money was going or our 8th-grade graduation party. I didn't answer. He said that he was going to call some of the people who pledged money to ask them if I had said anything about cancer.

"It was the only way I could raise enough money!" I answered back, knowing the lie had caught up with me.

"Well, it was the wrong thing to do." Principal Dorsey replied. "Now, you are going to have to contact every person who donated and let them know the truth. You also may not have enough money for a graduation party now."

I knew I should never have volunteered to lead this.

8. Part A
What sort of character is the narrator?

Ⓐ major
Ⓑ minor
Ⓒ middle
Ⓓ weak

8. Part B
Who or what is the antagonist in this story?

Ⓐ unnamed narrator
Ⓑ Abbie Morelle
Ⓒ Paulie Roman
Ⓓ none of the above

Understanding Slope (8.EE.B.6)

Day 3

1. **Which of the following statements is true about slope?**

    Ⓐ Slopes of straight lines will always be positive numbers.
    Ⓑ The slopes vary between the points on a straight line.
    Ⓒ Slope is determined by dividing the horizontal distance between two points by the corresponding vertical distance.
    Ⓓ Slope is determined by dividing the vertical distance between two points by the corresponding horizontal distance.

2. **Which of the following is an equation of the line passing through the points (-1, 4) and (1, 2)?**

    Ⓐ y = x - 3
    Ⓑ y = 2x + 2
    Ⓒ y = -2x + 4
    Ⓓ y = -x + 3

3. **The graph of which equation has the same slope as the graph of y = 4x + 3?**

    Ⓐ y = -2x + 3
    Ⓑ y = 2x - 3
    Ⓒ y = -4x + 2
    Ⓓ y = 4x - 2

4. **Find the slope between the points (-12, -5) and (0, 8).**

    Write your answer in the box given below.

Day 3

The Laundry

Charlie's parents always assigned him chores around the house. They would often ask him to trim the lawn, wash the dishes, and feed the dog. However, his chores never included laundry. He relied on his mother to wash his clothes for him. Charlie was an outstanding student and was recently accepted to a top college. The college he planned to attend was in New York City. Charlie was nervous about leaving Texas, where he grew up, and being so far away from his family; but, he knew that the college in New York was the perfect fit for him. Before he left, his mother decided that she had better show him how to wash his own clothes because she wouldn't be there to do it for him anymore. She showed Charlie how to sort his clothes into two piles: whites and colors.

Then she showed him how much soap to use and told him when to use hot or warm water and when to use cold water. Next, she explained the different settings on the dryer and told him to be careful not to dry certain items on high heat. Charlie didn't pay much attention. He didn't see what could happen or what was so complicated about washing clothes. He planned on packing mostly t-shirts and jeans and figured that it would be hard to mess up something so simple.

When Charlie arrived at school, he was completely overwhelmed with all of the exciting things to do and new people to meet. He was also careful to dedicate plenty of time to his schoolwork because he wanted to impress his professors and earn good grades. One morning Charlie woke up and found that he had no clean clothes to wear. His schedule had been so packed with activities and studying that he had managed to get through the first month of school without doing any laundry. That night, Charlie piled his soiled clothes into a large basket and headed to his dormitory's laundry room. He shoved all of his clothes into a washer, poured in the soap, and pressed the start. Half an hour later, he opened the washer and started moving the clothes into the dryer. It was then that he realized that he had skipped one very significant step. All of his white t-shirts and socks had turned pink. He had forgotten to sort his colors from his whites. Charlie had received a bright red t-shirt with his new school's logo across the front. The red dye had bled in the wash, turning all of his white clothes pink. Charlie was unhappy about his destroyed wardrobe, but he figured that there was absolutely nothing to do except to put the clothes in the dryer and hope for the best. So he transferred the clothes to a dryer and set the heat to high. After all, he was anxious to get back upstairs to his studies. An hour later, Charlie removed his clothes from the dryer and headed straight back to his dorm room. The following morning, he reached for one of his favorite t-shirts. It was slightly pink now, but he didn't have enough money to replace all of his newly pink clothes. He would have to wear them, pink or not. As he pulled the shirt over his head, he noticed that it seemed tight. He looked at himself in the mirror.

The shirt had shrunk in the dryer. It looked like he had tried to squeeze into his little sister's pink t-shirt. All Charlie could do was laugh. He called his mom and asked her to repeat her laundry instructions again.

This time, Charlie took notes.

5. Which statement best describes Charlie's parents' expectations of him?

Ⓐ They let Charlie do whatever he wants since he's smart and will probably make good decisions.
Ⓑ They expect Charlie to help around the house and earn good grades in school.
Ⓒ They don't expect much from Charlie since he probably won't fulfill their expectations.
Ⓓ They expect Charlie to do all the work around the house while earning straight A's.

6. Part A
What does this excerpt reveal about Charlie?

Ⓐ Charlie did not ask his mother for help with his clothes.
Ⓑ Charlie did not listen carefully to his mother's instructions on how to wash his clothes.
Ⓒ Charlie tried to enjoy doing his laundry.
Ⓓ Charlie is so eager to get his homework completed on time that he forgets the laundry instructions.

6. Part B
After Charlie had a mishap with his laundry, he laughed. What does this reveal about Charlie's character?

Ⓐ Charlie is the kind of person who realizes what's done is done; all he can do is try again.
Ⓑ Charlie is the kind of person who laughs wildly when he isn't sure how to react to stressful situations.
Ⓒ Charlie is the kind of person who laughs at the misfortune of others.
Ⓓ Charlie is the kind of person who laughs when he isn't sure what to do.

Excerpt from **Stave Five of A Christmas Carol** by Charles Dickens

(1) "What else can I be," returned the uncle [Scrooge], "when I live in such a world of fools as this? Merry Christmas! Out upon Merry Christmas! What's Christmas time to you but a time for paying bills without money; a time for finding yourself a year older, but not an hour richer; a time for balancing your books and having every item in 'em through a round dozen of months presented dead against you? If I could work my will," said Scrooge indignantly, "every idiot who goes about with 'Merry Christmas' on his lips should be boiled with his own pudding, and buried with a stake of holly through his heart. He should!"

Excerpt from **Stave Five of A Christmas Carol** by Charles Dickens

(2) "A merry Christmas, Bob!" said Scrooge [the uncle], with an earnestness that could not be mistaken, as he clapped him on the back. "A merrier Christmas, Bob, my good fellow, than I have given you, for many a year! I'll raise your salary, and endeavor to assist your struggling family, and we will discuss your affairs this very afternoon, over a Christmas bowl of smoking bishop, Bob! Make up the fires, and buy another coal-scuttle before you dot another, Bob Cratchit!"

"A merrier Christmas, Bob, my good fellow, than I have given you, for many a year! I'll raise your salary, and endeavor to assist your struggling family, and we will discuss your affairs this very afternoon, over a Christmas bowl of smoking bishop, Bob!

7. What is the significance of this dialogue?

Ⓐ This dialogue is significant because it shows that Scrooge wants to wish the person he's addressing a Merry Christmas.
Ⓑ This dialogue is significant because it is important for the reader to know Scrooge's feelings about Christmas.
Ⓒ This dialogue is significant because Scrooge wants to make sure everyone knows he dislikes Christmas.
Ⓓ This dialogue is significant because it shows Scrooge cannot wait for Christmas morning to come, so he can rip open his presents.

8. What is the most important purpose of this dialogue?

Ⓐ It allows the reader to really understand the change that Scrooge underwent in the story.
Ⓑ It allows the reader to see that Scrooge liked Christmas all along.
Ⓒ It allows the reader to see that nothing could change Scrooge's opinion of Christmas.
Ⓓ none of the above

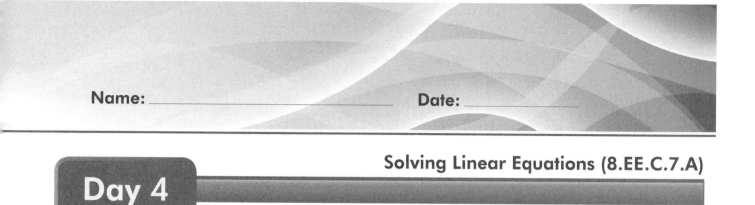

Day 4

1. Which two consecutive odd integers have a sum of 44?

   Ⓐ 21 and 23
   Ⓑ 19 and 21
   Ⓒ 23 and 25
   Ⓓ 17 and 19

2. During each of the first three quarters of the school year, Melissa earned a grade point average of 2.1, 2.9, and 3.1. What does her 4th quarter grade point average need to be in order to raise her grade to a 3.0 cumulative grade point average?

   Ⓐ 3.9
   Ⓑ 4.2
   Ⓒ 2.6
   Ⓓ 3.5

3. Martha is on a trip of 1,924 miles. She has already traveled 490 miles. She has 3 days left in her trip. How many miles does she need to travel each day to complete her trip?

   Ⓐ 450 miles/day
   Ⓑ 464 miles/day
   Ⓒ 478 miles/day
   Ⓓ 492 miles/day

4. Solve each equation for the variable. Select the ones whose values of the variables are the same.

   Note that more than one option may be correct. Select all the correct answers.

   Ⓐ $-5m = 25$
   Ⓑ $-10c = -80$
   Ⓒ $-7 + g = -12$
   Ⓓ $12m + 20 = -40$

Meaning and Tone (RL.8.4)

Day 4

5. What is the tone of a piece of literature?

- Ⓐ the rhythm of the words when read out loud
- Ⓑ the level of sound with which it should be read
- Ⓒ the author's attitude about the subject and/or the readers
- Ⓓ none of the above

6. What is the tone of this sentence?

Tonight's homework is to read thirty pages in the textbook.

- Ⓐ neutral
- Ⓑ dramatic
- Ⓒ angry
- Ⓓ friendly

7. What is the tone?

Oh great! My thoughtful teacher gave us homework again tonight! Sure, I have nothing better to do than read thirty pages out of an outdated textbook. I don't have a life.

- Ⓐ expectant
- Ⓑ sad
- Ⓒ sarcastic
- Ⓓ adoring

The Ungrateful Son
By Jacob and Wilhelm Grimm

Once a man was sitting with his wife before their front door. They had a roasted chicken which they were about to eat together. Then the man saw that his aged father was approaching, and he hastily took the chicken and hid it, for he did not want to share it with him. The old man came, had a drink, and went away. Now the son wanted to put the roasted chicken back onto the table, but when he reached for it, it had turned into a large toad, which jumped into his face and sat there and never went away again. If anyone tried to remove it, it looked venomously at him as though it would jump into his face, so that no one dared to touch it. And the ungrateful son was forced to feed the toad every day, or else it would eat from his face. And thus he went to and fro in the world without rest.

8. Part A
In this story, what does "hastily" most likely means?

- Ⓐ hurriedly
- Ⓑ slowly
- Ⓒ carefully
- Ⓓ quietly

8. Part B
In this story, "venomously" most closely means

- Ⓐ poisonous
- Ⓑ acting like a snake
- Ⓒ showing strong anger
- Ⓓ striking

Solve Linear Equations with Rational Numbers (8.EE.C.7.B)

Day 5

1. Solve the following linear equation: $\frac{7}{14} = n + \frac{7}{14}n$

    Ⓐ $n = 1\frac{1}{2}$

    Ⓑ $n = 3$

    Ⓒ $n = \frac{1}{3}$

    Ⓓ $n = 1$

2. Find the solution to the following equation: $2(2x - 7) = 14$

    Ⓐ $x = 14$
    Ⓑ $x = 7$
    Ⓒ $x = 1$
    Ⓓ $x = 0$

3. Solve the following equation for x.
    $6x - (2x + 5) = 11$

    Ⓐ $x = -3$
    Ⓑ $x = -4$
    Ⓒ $x = 3$
    Ⓓ $x = 4$

4. Select the ones that are correct.

    Note that more than one option may be correct.

    Ⓐ $w - \frac{2}{5} = \frac{8}{5}$ so $w = 2$

    Ⓑ $\frac{-5}{8}y = 15$ so $y = 24$

    Ⓒ $0.4x - 1.2 = 0.15x + 0.8$ so $x = 8$

    Ⓓ $\frac{x}{6} = -5$ so $x = 30$

Day 5

5. When you are comparing two things, what are you looking for?

   Ⓐ similarities
   Ⓑ differences
   Ⓒ similarities and differences
   Ⓓ none of the above

6. Which of the following group of signal words would you most likely find in a paper comparing two things?

   Ⓐ in addition, finally, above all
   Ⓑ meanwhile, coupled with, for instance
   Ⓒ likewise, as well, the same as
   Ⓓ although, however, contrary to

7. Which of the following graphic organizers is most effectively used to compare and contrast?

   Ⓐ Venn diagram
   Ⓑ brace map
   Ⓒ fish bone map
   Ⓓ tree map

The Mountain and The Squirrel	The Arrow and the Song
The mountain and the squirrel Had a quarrel; And the former called the latter, "Little Prig." Bun replied "You are doubtless very big; But all sorts of things and weather Must be taken in together To make up a year And a sphere.	I shot an arrow into the air It fellto earth, I knew not where; For, so swiftly it flew, the sight Could not follow it in its flight.
And I think it no disgrace To occupy my place. If I'm not so large as you, Your are not so small as I, And not half so spry; I'll not deny you make A very pretty squirrel track; Talents differ; all is well and wisely put; If I cannot carry forests on my back, Neither can you crack a nut" Ralph Waldo Emerson (1803 - 1882)	I breathed a song into the air It fell to earth, I knew not where For who has sight so keen and strong That it can follow the flight of song? Long, long afterward, in an oak I found the arrow, still unbroke And the song, from beginning to end I found again in the heart of a friend. H. W. Longfellow (1807 - 1882)

8. Part A
What is one comparison the reader can make about both poems?

Ⓐ Both the poems were written during the 19th century.
Ⓑ One of the poems was written in the 20th century.
Ⓒ Both the poems were written in the 20th century.
Ⓓ One of the poems was written in the 19th century.

8. Part B
One difference between the poems is _____.

Ⓐ dialogue
Ⓑ point of view
Ⓒ both A & B
Ⓓ none of the above

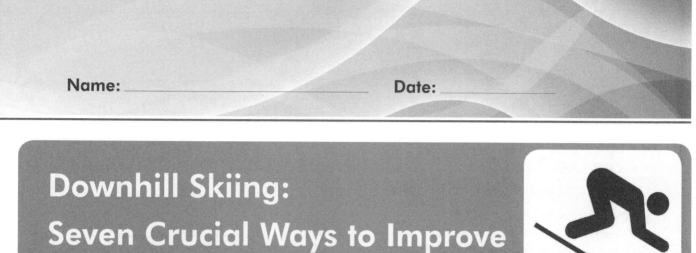

Downhill Skiing: Seven Crucial Ways to Improve Your Skills on the Slopes

Downhill Skiing is a sport that requires keen balance, powerful leg strength, and a bit of courage -- to say the least.

When first starting out, it can be a bit daunting for beginners to know where to start; not to mention the fear of falling and getting hurt. This guide will help any novice Downhill skier to improve their skills and become more confident with their abilities on the mountain.

1. Improve Your Balance

As you might imagine, balance is a fundamental skill to have for any skier: if you can't balance well, you won't go far in the sport.

While you might be able to balance on one leg when standing, it is a completely different story when you are sliding down a hill with long planks attached to your boots.

Although it might not be the funniest thing to do, drills on flat ground or the "bunny hill" will help you improve your balance.

To start, you can try the "balance on one side drill", whereby you stand on one ski, lift your other foot off the ground, and propel yourself forward with your poles -- using what is called the double pull (pushing down on both poles simultaneously).

Do this for thirty seconds or so then switch legs. You'll find that over time, your stability will gradually improve.

2. Build Strength in your Upper Legs

The constant maneuvering necessary when skiing will make even the strongest legs feel like noodles. To last longer on the hills and become more powerful on the powder, you should strengthen your legs by doing squats.

Start standing with your feet shoulder-width apart. Let your body drop slowly while keeping your weight on your heels, your hips back, and your back straight and at a slight forward angle.

Continue as deep as you can, ensuring that your nose, knees, and toes are constantly in alignment. Do the reverse and push yourself back up, maintaining the same form, and repeat as many times as you can. Although your legs will burn, push past the pain for best results.

3. Increase your Calf Endurance

Calve-ups are a great way to make your calves more muscular. Simply find some stairs or a ledge and stand with heel hanging off the edge.

Week 2 Online Activity

Login to the Lumos student account and complete the following activities.

1. Reading assignment
2. Vocabulary practice
3. Write your summer diary

If you haven't created your Lumos account, use the URL and access code below to get started.

URL: http://www.lumoslearning.com/a/tedbooks

Access Code: G8-9MLSLH-73851

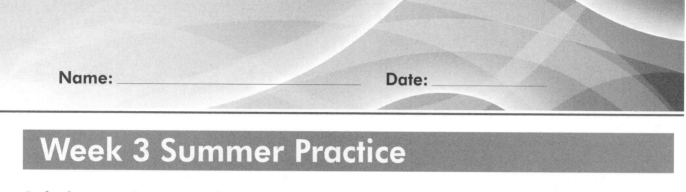

Week 3 Summer Practice

Solutions to Systems of Equations (8.EE.C.8.A)

Day 1

1. Which of the following points is the intersection of the graphs of the lines given by the equations y = x - 5 and y = 2x + 1 ?

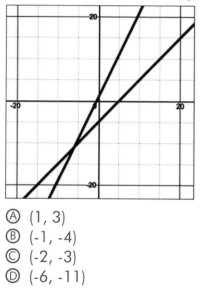

   Ⓐ (1, 3)
   Ⓑ (-1, -4)
   Ⓒ (-2, -3)
   Ⓓ (-6, -11)

2. Which of the following describes the solution set of this system?

   y = 0.5x + 7
   y = 0.5x - 1

   Ⓐ The solution is (-2, -3) because the graphs of the two equations intersect at that point.
   Ⓑ The solution is (0.5, 3) because the graphs of the two equations intersect at that point.
   Ⓒ There is no solution because the graphs of the two equations are parallel lines.
   Ⓓ There are infinitely many solutions because the graphs of the two equations are the same line.

3. Find the solution to the following system:

y = 2(2 - 3x);
y = -3(2x + 3)

Ⓐ x = -1; y = 10
Ⓑ x = -2; y = 24
Ⓒ x = -3; y = 22
Ⓓ There is no solution.

4. Randy has to raise $50.00 to repair his bicycle. He is only $1.00 short. He has only $1 and $5 bills. If he has one more $1 bills than $5 bills, how many does he have of each?

Circle the correct answer choice.

Ⓐ Ten $1-bills, Nine $5-bills
Ⓑ Nine $1-bills and Eight $5-bills
Ⓒ Eight $1-bills and Seven $5-bills
Ⓓ Seven $1-bills and Six $5-bills

Day 1

5. **Which of the following is an example of a pun?**

   Ⓐ A boiled egg every morning is hard to beat.
   Ⓑ Nicholas went to buy some camouflage pants the other day, but he couldn't find any.
   Ⓒ Our social studies teacher says her globe means the world to her.
   Ⓓ all of the above

6. **What literary elements can add humor to a story?**

   Ⓐ pun
   Ⓑ setting or situation
   Ⓒ irony
   Ⓓ all of the above

7. **What is the best definition of irony?**

   Ⓐ interesting dialogue between characters
   Ⓑ a scene in which something is complex and difficult to understand
   Ⓒ surprising, funny, or interesting contradictions
   Ⓓ a line that is straight to the point

The Tempest, Act III, Scene II [Be not afeard]

William Shakespeare, 1564 - 1616

Caliban speaks to Stephano and Trinculo.

Be not afeard; the isle is full of noises,
Sounds and sweet airs, that give delight, and hurt not.
Sometimes a thousand twangling instruments
Will hum about mine ears; and sometime voices,
That, if I then had waked after long sleep,
Will make me sleep again: and then, in dreaming,
The clouds methought would open, and show riches
Ready to drop upon me; that, when I waked,
I cried to dream again.

8. Describe what not to be afraid of? Write your answer in the box below.

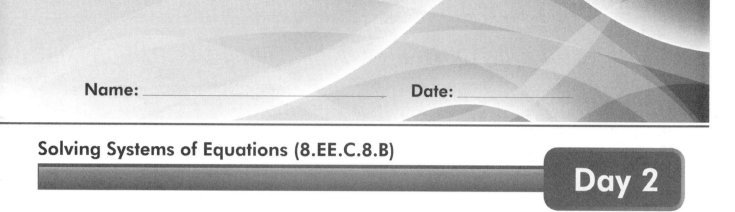

Solving Systems of Equations (8.EE.C.8.B)

Day 2

1. Find the solution to the following system of equations:
   $13x + 3y = 15$ and $y = 5 - 4x$.

   Ⓐ $x = 0, y = 5$
   Ⓑ $x = 5, y = 0$
   Ⓒ $x = 9, y = -31$
   Ⓓ All real numbers are solutions.

2. Solve the system:
   $y = 2x + 5$
   $y = 3x - 7$

   Ⓐ $x = 12, y = 29$
   Ⓑ $x = 3, y = 11$
   Ⓒ $x = 5, y = -2$
   Ⓓ $x = -1, y = 3$

3. Solve the system:
   $2x + 3y = 14$
   $2x - 3y = -10$

   Ⓐ $x = 1, y = 4$
   Ⓑ $x = 2, y = 12$
   Ⓒ $x = 4, y = 2$
   Ⓓ $x = 10, y = 10$

4. Which of these will have one solution?

Note that more than one option may be correct. Select all the correct answers.

Ⓐ $y = \dfrac{3}{4}x + 1$
$y = -\dfrac{1}{2}x - 4$

Ⓑ $y = -3x + 2$
$3x + y = -4$

Ⓒ $y = \dfrac{1}{3}x - 3$
$2x + y = 4$

Ⓓ $-x + 2y = -2$
$4y = 2x - 4$

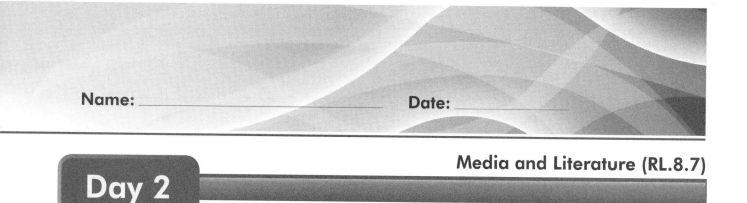
Day 2

Casey Jones
A Tennessee Legend retold by S.E. Schlosser

Casey Jones, that heroic railroad engineer of the Cannonball, was known as the man who always brought the train in on time. He would blow the whistle, so it started off soft but would increase to a wail louder than a banshee before dying off so that people would recognize that whistle and know when Casey was driving past.

April 29, 1900, Casey brought the Cannonball into Memphis dead on time. As he was leaving, he found out one of the other engineers was sick and unable to make his run. So Casey volunteered to help out his friend. He pulled the train out of the station about eleven p.m., an hour and thirty-five minutes late. Casey was determined to make up the time. As soon as he could, he highballed out of Memphis (highballing means to go very fast and take a lot of risks to get where you are headed) and started making up for the lost time.

About four a.m., when he had nearly made up all the time on the run, Casey rounded a corner near Vaughn, Mississippi, and saw a stalled freight train on the track. He shouted for his fireman to jump. The fireman made it out alive, but Casey Jones died in the wreck, one hand on the brake and one on the whistle chord.

5. **What medium of publication would be best to use if you wanted to make it possible for people to see Casey Jones operating the train?**

   Ⓐ a video
   Ⓑ digital text
   Ⓒ a traditional book
   Ⓓ none of the above

6. **What are the advantages of using media to present a particular topic or idea?**

   Ⓐ It can create a picture for viewers to see
   Ⓑ It provides a clear voice for viewers to hear
   Ⓒ both A and B
   Ⓓ none of the above

7. **If you want to see one person's visual interpretation of a character's appearance, what medium of publication would be best to use?**

Ⓐ movie version of a text
Ⓑ print text
Ⓒ digital text
Ⓓ none of the above

The Lake Isle of Innisfree

I will arise and go now, and go to Innisfree,
And a small cabin build there, of clay and wattles made:
Nine bean-rows will I have there, a hive for the honey-bee;
And live alone in the bee-loud glade.
And I shall have some peace there, for peace comes dropping slow,
Dropping from the veils of the morning to where the cricket sings;
There midnight's all a glimmer, and noon a purple glow,
And evening full of the linnet's wings.
I will arise and go now, for always night and day
I hear lake water lapping with low sounds by the shore;
While I stand on the roadway, or on the pavements grey,
I hear it in the deep heart's core.
W. B. Yeats

About the poet:
William Butler Yeats was an Irish poet and a dramatist. He was one of the foremost figures of 20th-century literature and was the driving force behind the Irish literary revival. Together with Lady Gregory and Edward Martin, Yeats founded the Abbey Theater. He served as its chief during its early years and was a pillar of the Irish literary establishment in his later years.

The above well-known poem explores the poet's longing for the peace and tranquility of Innisfree, a place where he spent a lot of time as a boy. This poem is a lyric.

image obtained from freephotosbank.com

8. Part A
Which medium of publication, the poem or the picture, gives you a better visualization of the lake?

Ⓐ the picture
Ⓑ the poem
Ⓒ neither
Ⓓ both

8. Part B
Which medium of publication, the poem or the picture, appeals to more than one of the five senses?

Ⓐ the picture
Ⓑ the poem
Ⓒ neither
Ⓓ both

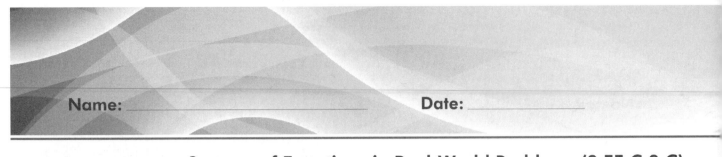

Day 3

Systems of Equations in Real-World Problems (8.EE.C.8.C)

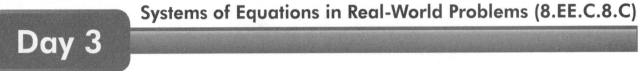

1. Jorge and Jillian have cell phones with different service providers. Jorge pays $50 a month and $1 per text message sent. Jillian pays $72 a month and $0.12 per text message sent. How many texts would each of them have to send in order for their bill to be the same amount at the end of the month?

   Ⓐ 2 texts
   Ⓑ 22 texts
   Ⓒ 25 texts
   Ⓓ 47 texts

2. Mr. Stevens is 63 years older than his grandson, Tom. In 3 years, Mr. Stevens will be four times as old as Tom. How old is Tom?

   Ⓐ 17 years
   Ⓑ 18 years
   Ⓒ 20 years
   Ⓓ 22 years

3. Janet has packed a total of 50 textbooks and workbooks in a box, but she can't remember how many of each are in the box. Each textbook weighs 2 pounds, and each workbook weighs 0.5 pounds, and the total weight of the books in the box is 55 pounds. If t is the number of textbooks and w is the number of workbooks, which of the following systems of equations represents this situation?

   Ⓐ $t + w = 55$
       $2t + 0.5w = 50$

   Ⓑ $2t + w = 50$
       $t + 0.5w = 55$

   Ⓒ $t + w = 50$
       $2t + 0.5w = 55$

   Ⓓ $t + w = 55$
       $2.5(t + w) = 50$

4. The admission fee at a carnival is \$3.00 for children and \$5.00 for adults. On the first day 1,500 people enter the fair and \$5740 is collected. How many children and how many adults attended the carnival?

Select the correct system and answer. There can be more than one correct answer, choose all applicable ones.

Ⓐ $\begin{cases} 3c + 5a = 1500 \\ c + a = 5740 \end{cases}$

Ⓑ $\begin{cases} 3c + 5a = 5740 \\ c + a = 1500 \end{cases}$

Ⓒ a=620, c=880

Ⓓ a=936 c=564

Modern Fictions and Traditional Stories (RL.8.9)

Day 3

5. What is a motif?

- Ⓐ the major characters in the story
- Ⓑ how the story ends
- Ⓒ the plot
- Ⓓ a recurring element or idea in a story

6. Which of the following is a popular motif in traditional stories?

- Ⓐ good vs. evil
- Ⓑ a test of courage
- Ⓒ children who are heroes
- Ⓓ all of the above

The Ant and the Grasshopper
Aesop's Fable

In a field, one summer's day, a grasshopper was hopping about, chirping and singing to its heart's content. A group of ants walked by, grunting as they struggled to carry plump kernels of corn. "Where are you going with those heavy things?" asked the grasshopper.

Without stopping, the first ant replied, "To our anthill. This is the third kernel I've delivered today." "Why not come and sing with me," teased the grasshopper, "instead of working so hard?" "We are helping to store food for the winter," said the ant, "and think you should do the same." "Winter is far away, and it is a glorious day to play," sang the grasshopper. But the ants went on their way and continued their hard work.

The weather soon turned cold. All the food lying in the field was covered with a thick white blanket of snow that even the grasshopper could not dig through.

Soon the grasshopper found itself dying of hunger. He staggered to the ants' hill and saw them handing out corn from the stores they had collected in the summer. He begged them for something to eat. "What!" cried the ants in surprise, "haven't you stored anything away for the winter? What in the world were you doing all last summer?"

"I didn't have time to store any food," complained the grasshopper; "I was so busy playing music that before I knew it, the summer was gone."

The ants shook their heads in disgust, turned their backs on the grasshopper, and went on with their work.

7. What is the lesson of this fable?

 Ⓐ It's okay to have fun.
 Ⓑ Do not help those around you.
 Ⓒ Work hard to prepare for the future.
 Ⓓ Listen to what you are told.

8. "When someone declares an event to be a ""modern day Cinderella story"" they mean _____.

Fill in the blank after selecting the correct answer choice from the 4 options given below."

 Ⓐ someone poor or common becomes successful
 Ⓑ someone has evil step-sisters
 Ⓒ someone rides a carriage
 Ⓓ someone is the most beautiful in her family

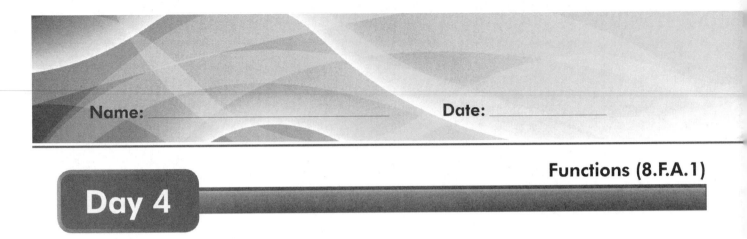
Day 4

1. Which of the following is NOT a function?

- Ⓐ {(2, 3), (4, 7), (8, 6)}
- Ⓑ {(2, 2), (4, 4), (8, 8)}
- Ⓒ {(2, 3), (4, 3), (8, 3)}
- Ⓓ {(2, 3), (2, 7), (8, 6)}

2. Which of the following tables shows that y is a function of x?

Ⓐ
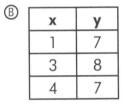

x	y
1	4
1	7
4	7

Ⓑ
x	y
1	7
3	8
4	7

Ⓒ
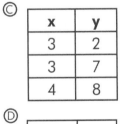

x	y
3	2
3	7
4	8

Ⓓ
x	y
1	7
4	7
4	9

3. If y is a function of x, which of the following CANNOT be true?

Ⓐ A particular x value is associated with two different y values.
Ⓑ Two different x values are associated with the same y value.
Ⓒ Every x value is associated with the same y value.
Ⓓ Every x value is associated with a different y value.

4. Select the sets of ordered pairs that represent a function.

There can be more than one correct option. Select all the correct options.

Ⓐ {(1, 1), (2, 2), (3, 3), (4, 4)}
Ⓑ {(1, -2), (-2, 0), (-1, 2), (1, 3)}
Ⓒ {(-2, 3), (0, 1), (2, -1), (3, -2)}
Ⓓ {(-1, 7), (0, -3), (1, 10), (0, 7)}

Making Inferences Based on Textual Evidence (RI.8.1)

Day 4

5. What is an inference?

- Ⓐ an answer that is clearly stated in the text
- Ⓑ a logical conclusion drawn from evidence in a text
- Ⓒ an opinion made from reading a text
- Ⓓ a direct quotation found in the text

6. What is the proper way to make a direct citation from a text?

- Ⓐ put the citation in italics
- Ⓑ underline the citation
- Ⓒ put the citation in quotes
- Ⓓ make the citation bold

7. What is the best way to cite evidence from a text?

- Ⓐ summarize
- Ⓑ paraphrase
- Ⓒ in quotes
- Ⓓ all of the above

Stephen and Joseph Montgolfier were papermakers, but they had been interested in flying for many years. One night, in 1782, Joseph noticed something that gave him an idea. He was sitting in front of the fire when he saw some small pieces of scorched paper being carried up the chimney.

Soon afterwards, the brothers conducted an experiment. They lit a fire under a small silk bag, which was open at the bottom; at once, the bag rose to the ceiling. After this, Stephen and Joseph conducted many more experiments, both indoors and in the open air. Eventually, they built a huge balloon of linen and paper. On June 5th, 1783, they launched their balloon in the village of Annonay.

8. **Part A**
Which specific detail in the above passage describes the first experiment the brothers did?

Ⓐ Stephen and Joseph Montgolfier were papermakers, but they had been interested in flying for many years.

Ⓑ He was sitting in front of the fire when he saw some small pieces of scorched paper being carried up the chimney.

Ⓒ After this, Stephen and Joseph conducted many more experiments, both indoors and in the open air.

Ⓓ They lit a fire under a small silk bag, which was open at the bottom; at once, the bag rose to the ceiling.

8. **Part B**
The reader can tell from the article that Joseph Montgolfier was very observant because

Ⓐ He created a balloon from paper and linen.

Ⓑ He noticed the small pieces of burnt paper being carried up the chimney.

Ⓒ He found the best location to launch the balloon.

Ⓓ He was interested in flying.

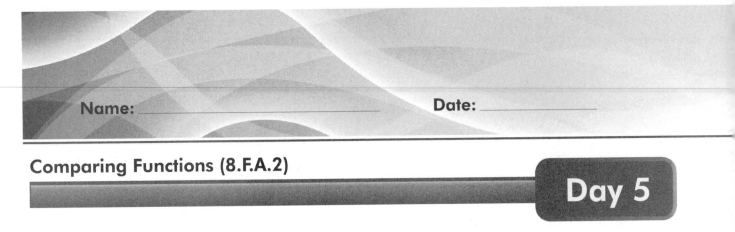

Comparing Functions (8.F.A.2)

Day 5

1. A set of instructions says to subtract 5 from a number n and then double that result, calling the final result p. Which function rule represents this set of instructions?

   Ⓐ p = 2(n – 5)
   Ⓑ p = 2n – 5
   Ⓒ n = 2(p – 5)
   Ⓓ n = 2p – 5

2. Which of the following linear functions is represented by the (x, y) pairs shown in the table below?

x	y
-3	-1
1	7
4	13

   Ⓐ y = x + 2
   Ⓑ y = 2x + 5
   Ⓒ y = 3x + 1
   Ⓓ y = 4x + 3

3.

x	y
0	3
1	5
2	7

   Three (x, y) pairs of a linear function are shown in the table above. Which of the following functions has the same slope as the function shown in the table?

   Ⓐ y = 3x + 2
   Ⓑ y = 2x -4
   Ⓒ y = x + 3
   Ⓓ y = x - 1

4. Put the correct inequality or equality sign between the rates of change of the two functions given below.

    Instruction : Take f to be the first function {(0, 0), (3, 180), (6, 360), (9, 540)} and g to be the second function y = 100x

    {(0, 0), (3, 180), (6, 360), (9, 540)} [   ] y = 100x

Day 5

5. What is a central idea?

Ⓐ the idea stated in the topic sentence
Ⓑ the theme of a piece of literature
Ⓒ who a piece of informational text is mainly about
Ⓓ the main idea of a piece of informational text

6. What statement is true about a central idea?

Ⓐ It can sometimes be found in the title of the text.
Ⓑ It is supported by the details in the text.
Ⓒ It covers the whole text.
Ⓓ all of the above

7. When determining the central idea of a text, it is important not to confuse it with:

Ⓐ the topic
Ⓑ the details
Ⓒ none of the above
Ⓓ both A & B

Name: _____   Date: _____

Learning how to ride a bike is no easy task. Most people learn as children and mount their first bicycle with training wheels mounted on the sides of the back tires. Those training wheels eventually come off. When that happens, usually someone runs behind the bicycle, holding the back of the seat as the rider learns to balance on two wheels. As the runner runs back and forth down the street, the rider eventually picks up on how to lean to stay up on two wheels. Eventually, the runner lets go of the seat, and the rider rides off on his or her own.

8. "What is the central idea of this passage? Circle the correct answer choice."

Ⓐ learning how to run behind a new rider
Ⓑ how to take training wheels off a bicycle
Ⓒ learning how to ride a two wheel bicycle
Ⓓ none of the above

Draw and Color

Draw and Color

Week 4 Summer Practice

Linear Functions (8.F.A.3)

Day 1

1. A linear function includes the ordered pairs (2, 5), (6, 7), and (k, 11). What is the value of k?

   Ⓐ 8
   Ⓑ 10
   Ⓒ 12
   Ⓓ 14

2. Which of the following functions is NOT linear?

   Ⓐ $f(x) = x + 0.5$
   Ⓑ $f(x) = -x + 0.5$
   Ⓒ $f(x) = x^2 + 0.5$
   Ⓓ $f(x) = 0.5x$

3. Which of the following functions is linear and includes the point (3, 0)?

   Ⓐ $f(x) = 3/x$
   Ⓑ $f(x) = x - 3$
   Ⓒ $f(x) = 3$
   Ⓓ $f(x) = 3x$

4. Write whether this represents a linear or non-linear function.

   $2x^2 + 3y = 10$

Day 1

5. What does it mean to make a distinction?

- Ⓐ to find a similarity
- Ⓑ to find a difference
- Ⓒ to draw a conclusion
- Ⓓ to point out a fact

6. What does it mean to make a connection?

- Ⓐ to find a similarity
- Ⓑ to find a difference
- Ⓒ to draw a conclusion
- Ⓓ to point out a fact

Archaeology is the study of past human life and culture through systematically examining and interpreting the material remains left behind. These material remains include archaeological sites (e.g., settlements, building features, graves), as well as cultural materials or artifacts such as tools and pottery. Through the interpretation and classification of archaeological materials, archaeologists work to understand past human behavior. In some countries, archaeology is often historical or art historical, with a strong emphasis on Culture history, archaeological sites, and artifacts such as art objects. In the New World, archaeology can be either a part of history and classical studies or anthropology.

The exact origins of archaeology as a discipline are uncertain. Excavations of ancient monuments and the collection of antiquities have been taking place for thousands of years. It was only in the 19th century, however, that the systematic study of the past through its physical remains underwent professionalization, which meant it began to be carried out in a manner recognizable to modern students of archaeology.

7. What is similar between New World archeology and archeology of the past?

- Ⓐ They both focus on history.
- Ⓑ They both focus on art.
- Ⓒ They both focus on culture.
- Ⓓ all of the above

Marathon

Training for a marathon takes hard work and perseverance. It is not something you can do on the spur of the moment. Preparing for a marathon takes months, particularly if you have never run a marathon before. The official distance of a full marathon is 26.2 miles. In 2005, the average time to complete a marathon in the United States was 4 hours 32 minutes 8 seconds for men and 5 hours 6 minutes 8 seconds for women.

Most people who run marathons are not trying to win. Many runners try to beat their own best time. Some compare their time to other runners in the same gender and age group. Some people set time-oriented goals, such as finishing under four hours, while others try to complete the race without slowing to a walk. Many beginners simply hope to finish the marathon.

Trainers recommend that beginners maintain a consistent running schedule for six weeks prior to even starting a marathon training program. The purpose of this is to allow the body to adapt to the various physical demands of long-distance running. First-time marathon runners should train by running four days a week for at least four months, increasing distance by no more than ten percent weekly. As race day approaches, runners should taper their runs, reducing the strain on their bodies and resting before the marathon. It is important not to overexert yourself during training because that can lead to a lot of injuries. Most common injuries are spraining of the knees and ankles. These sprains can hinder the training.

Before the race, it is important to stretch in order to keep muscles limber. Staying hydrated is also important, but there is a danger in drinking too much water. If a runner drinks too much water, they may experience a dangerous condition called hyponatremia, a drop of sodium levels in the blood. So only drink water when you are thirsty. During the race, trainers recommend maintaining a steady pace. It is normal to feel sore after a marathon. Light exercise will help sore muscles heal faster.

Some people run marathons in pairs or groups. Training for and running a marathon with another person or group of people can make the experience more enjoyable and more rewarding. A running partner might be just the motivation you need to show up for an early morning run instead of rolling over to hit the snooze button. And, when you cross the finish line together, you can share the satisfaction of reaching your common goal.

Usually, thousands of people sign up and run a Marathon. Most people finish the race. The thrill of running a marathon for the first time is unbelievable. The training sessions are harder if you have never run before. But it is unbelievable what ones' body can do when one puts their mind to it. Having a good coach to support you makes all the difference in training for a marathon.

The daily runs are very important. Strength training and core training are also very important.

The health benefits you gain from training are tremendous. Your core muscles grow stronger, and you will have tighter thighs and gluts. Your heart will be much stronger, and you can maintain lower cholesterol and blood sugar levels. Overall, you will look better and become healthier.

Nothing can explain how people feel when they reach that finish line at the end of the race. All the hard work and months of training feel worthwhile. The feeling of accomplishing something great overtakes you. It is great to run a marathon, but it is even greater to finish it.

8. Part A
How is a marathon competition different than most competitions?

Ⓐ Runners compete against themselves to beat past times.
Ⓑ Runners do not compete against each other.
Ⓒ Runners set their own personal records.
Ⓓ all of the above

8. Part B
What makes marathon running similar to other competitive sports?

Ⓐ health benefits
Ⓑ trophies
Ⓒ winning
Ⓓ numbers of people

Day 2

Linear Function Models (8.F.B.4)

1. If a graph includes the points (2, 5) and (8, 5), which of the following must be true?

   Ⓐ It is the graph of a linear function.
   Ⓑ It is the graph of an increasing function.
   Ⓒ It is not the graph of a function.
   Ⓓ None of the above

2. The graph of a linear function y = mx + 2 goes through the point (4, 0). Which of the following must be true?

   Ⓐ m is negative.
   Ⓑ m = 0
   Ⓒ m is positive
   Ⓓ Cannot be determined.

3. The graph of a linear function y = 2x + b passes through the point (-5, 0). Which of the following must be true?

   Ⓐ b is positive.
   Ⓑ b is negative.
   Ⓒ b = 0
   Ⓓ Cannot be determined.

4. Match each slope and coordinates of point with the correct equation

	y=−4x−3	y=7x-5	y=-x+2
(1, 2) slope=7	○	○	○
(-2, 5) slope=-4	○	○	○
(3, -1) slope=-1	○	○	○

Determining Meaning of Words(RI.8.4)

Day 2

5. What is connotation?

    Ⓐ a dictionary definition
    Ⓑ what a word means based on its context in a story
    Ⓒ a word with multiple meanings
    Ⓓ an opinion based on fact

6. What is denotation?

    Ⓐ a dictionary definition
    Ⓑ what a word means based on its context in a story
    Ⓒ a word that has a meaning that has changed over time
    Ⓓ an opinion based on fact

The Emperor Penguin is the only penguin species that breeds during the Antarctic winter. It treks 31–75 miles over the ice to breeding colonies, which may include thousands of penguins. The female lays a single egg, which is then incubated by the male while the female returns to the sea to feed; parents subsequently take turns foraging at sea and caring for their chick in the colony. The average lifespan of the Empire Penguin is 20 years, although observations suggest that some Emperor Penguins may live to 50 years of age.

7. Based on how the word "trek" is used in the passage, determine its meaning.

    Ⓐ to fly a long distance
    Ⓑ to circulate in a specific area
    Ⓒ to walk a long distance
    Ⓓ to live a long life

From Chapter 2 of **Bullets and Billets** by Bruce Bainsfather

I stood in a queue of Gordons, Seaforths, Worcesters, etc., slowly moving up one, until, finally arriving at the companion (nearly said staircase), I tobogganed down into the hold, and spent what was left of the night dealing out those rations. Having finished, at last, I came to the surface again, and now, as the transport glided along through the dirty waters of the river, and as I gazed at the motley collection of Frenchmen on the various wharves, and saw a variety of soldiery, and a host of other warlike "props," I felt acutely that now I was in the war at last—the real thing! For some time, I had been rehearsing in England; but that was over now, and here I was—in the common or garden vernacular—"in the soup."

8. Part A
Based on how they are used to begin the passage, what are "Gordons, Seaforths, and Worcesters?

Ⓐ ranks in an army
Ⓑ types of holding facilities on a ship
Ⓒ different destinations on the journey
Ⓓ none of the above

8. Part B
The author is using what type of figurative language to compare war to a theater in the above passage.

Ⓐ implied metaphor
Ⓑ simile
Ⓒ imagery
Ⓓ allusion

Day 3

1. **Complete the following:**
   The cost per copy is a function of the number of copies of any one title purchased. This implies that _____

   Ⓐ the cost per copy of any one title is always a constant.
   Ⓑ the cost per copy of any one title will change based on the number of copies purchased.
   Ⓒ the cost per copy of any one title is not related to the number of copies purchased.
   Ⓓ None of the above.

2. **If a student's math grade is a positive function of the number of hours he spends preparing for a test, which of the following is correct?**

   Ⓐ The more he studies, the lower his grade.
   Ⓑ The more he studies, the higher his grade.
   Ⓒ There is no relation between how much he studies and his grade.
   Ⓓ The faster he finishes his work, the higher his grade will be.

3. **Mandy took a math quiz and received an initial score of i. She retook the quiz several times and, with each attempt, doubled her previous score.**
   After a TOTAL of four attempts, her final score was _____.

   Ⓐ 2i
   Ⓑ 3i
   Ⓒ 2^3i
   Ⓓ None of the above.

4. Observe the graph given.
   Match each segment to whether it is increasing or decreasing as per the graph.

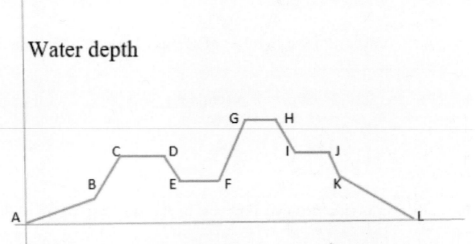

	INCREASING	DECREASING	CONSTANT
A to B	○	○	○
B to C	○	○	○
G to H	○	○	○
I to J	○	○	○
J to K	○	○	○
K to L	○	○	○
C to D	○	○	○
E to F	○	○	○
D to E	○	○	○
F to G	○	○	○
H to I	○	○	○

Analyzing Structures in Text (RI.8.4)

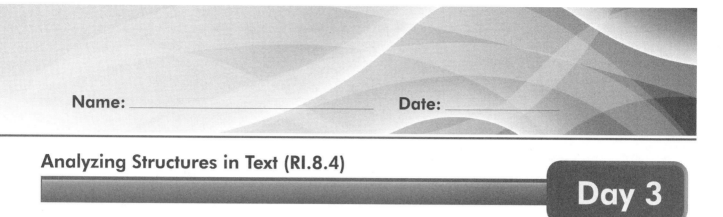

Day 3

5. What should you look at when analyzing the structure of a piece of text?

   Ⓐ the genre of writing
   Ⓑ the author's purpose
   Ⓒ the types of transition words that are being used
   Ⓓ all of the above

6. What type of writing has the following literary elements: characters, conflict, setting, and plot?

   Ⓐ nonfiction
   Ⓑ fiction
   Ⓒ technical
   Ⓓ poetry

7. If you saw words such as, "unlike", "as well as", "on the other hand", and "in contrast", what would you think the author's purpose was?

   Ⓐ to persuade
   Ⓑ to compare
   Ⓒ to entertain
   Ⓓ wouldn't be able to tell

Archaeology	History of Mankind
Archaeology is the study of past human life and culture through systematically examining and interpreting the material remains left behind. These material remains include archaeological sites (e.g., settlements, building features, graves), as well as cultural materials or artifacts such as tools and pottery. Through the interpretation and classification of archaeological materials, archaeologists work to understand past human behavior. In some countries, archaeology is often historical or art historical, with a strong emphasis on cultural history, archaeological sites, and artifacts such as art objects. In the New World, archaeology can be either a part of history and classical studies or anthropology. The exact origins of archaeology as a discipline are uncertain. Excavations of ancient monuments and the collection of antiquities have been taking place for thousands of years. It was only in the 19th century, however, that the systematic study of the past through its physical remains began to be carried out in a manner recognizable to modern students of archaeology.	History is about events that happened in the past. It is like an interesting and exciting series of stories. However, these stories are not like the many fairy tales you may have read. These stories are about real people and events that have really happened. It tells us about the lives of great men_ Some were great rulers who fought battles and conquered lands. Some were famous teachers, writers, explorers, scientists, artists, and musicians. They performed great deeds and showed people how to lead productive lives. History tells us how early civilization began. It describes how those people lived, how they got their food, and how they built their villages and cities. How do we have a record of events from long ago? In recent years. People have excavated ruins of old cities that were buried deep beneath the ground. We can learn about the people who lived in the lost cities by carefully examining artifacts found in these sites. Some of the items include sharp stones used for hunting, pots, and pans used for cooking and beads and necklaces used as jewelry. These items offer some clues about the life of people who lived during that time.

8. **Part A**
Both passages focus on _____.

Ⓐ the method of finding artifacts.
Ⓑ learning more about the past.
Ⓒ why history is taught in school.
Ⓓ events in history.

8. **Part B**
What comparison can be made between the two passages?

Ⓐ Both passages are about human life in the past.
Ⓑ Both passages are about mummies.
Ⓒ Both A and B.
Ⓓ None of the above.

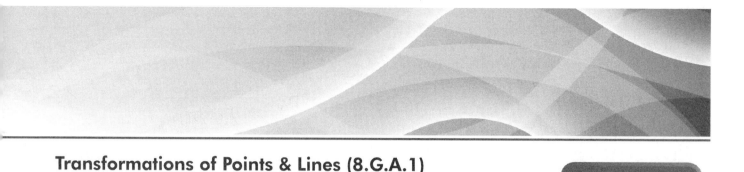

Transformations of Points & Lines (8.G.A.1)

Day 4

1. The point (4, 3) is rotated 90° clockwise about the origin. What are the coordinates of the resulting point?

    Ⓐ (-3, 4)
    Ⓑ (-4, 3)
    Ⓒ (4, -3)
    Ⓓ (3, -4)

2. A line segment has a length of 9 units. After a certain transformation is applied to the segment, the new segment has a length of 9 units. What was the transformation?

    Ⓐ A rotation
    Ⓑ A reflection
    Ⓒ A translation
    Ⓓ Any of the above transformations.

3. The point (2, 4) is rotated 180° clockwise about the origin. What are the coordinates of the resulting point?

    Ⓐ (-2, -4)
    Ⓑ (-2, 4)
    Ⓒ (2, -4)
    Ⓓ (2, 4)

4. Enter the correct operation that will describe the rule for the translation left 3 units and up 4 units?

    $(x, y) \rightarrow (x \boxed{} 3, y \boxed{} 4)$

Day 4

5. What is point of view?

Ⓐ a character's view of the action in a story
Ⓑ the perspective from which a story is told
Ⓒ where the author is when writing a story
Ⓓ the view of the character in the story

6. Which type of point of view uses the pronouns, "I" "me" and "my"?

Ⓐ first person
Ⓑ third person omniscient
Ⓒ third person limited
Ⓓ second person

7. When the narrator is one of the characters in the story, what point of view is the story being told from?

Ⓐ First person
Ⓑ Third person omniscient
Ⓒ Third person limited
Ⓓ second person

8. "Often when reading a magazine you will come across advertisements. These advertisements are meant to:

Circle the correct answer choice."

Ⓐ show the reader a product
Ⓑ persuade the reader to buy the product
Ⓒ introduce the reader to the product
Ⓓ provide the reader with a break from stories

Day 5

1. ΔABC is reflected across the x-axis.
   Which two angles are equivalent?

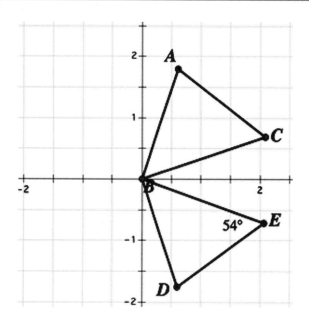

   Ⓐ ∠A and ∠C
   Ⓑ ∠A and ∠E
   Ⓒ ∠C and ∠D
   Ⓓ ∠C and ∠E

2. ΔABC is rotated 90°.
   Which two angles are equivalent?

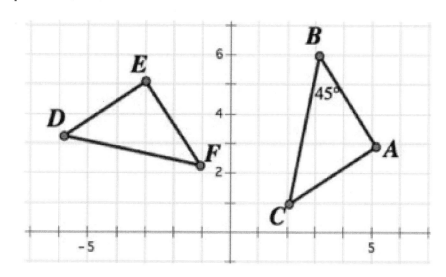

   Ⓐ ∠A and ∠C
   Ⓑ ∠B and ∠E
   Ⓒ ∠C and ∠D
   Ⓓ ∠C and ∠F

3. What rigid transformation should be used to prove angle ∠ABC ≅ ∠XYZ?

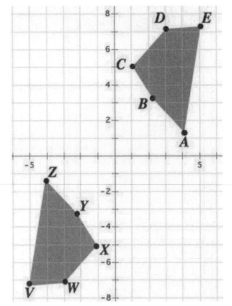

Ⓐ Reflection
Ⓑ Rotation
Ⓒ Translation
Ⓓ None of the above

4. Select the angle measure that corresponds with each transformation. Your preimage has an angle measure of 30°

	30°	60°	90°
Translation	○	○	○
Reflection	○	○	○
Rotation	○	○	○
Dilation	○	○	○

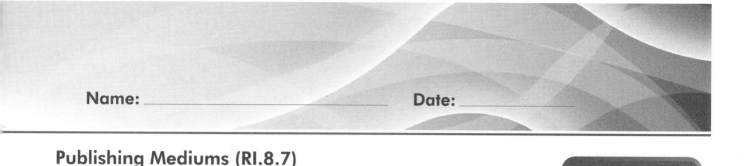
Publishing Mediums (RI.8.7)

Day 5

5. Which of the following is important to consider when reading a text online?

    Ⓐ evaluate the background of the source
    Ⓑ look for why the information is being provided
    Ⓒ check the date of the source
    Ⓓ all of the above

6. You want to write a short piece that people can respond to immediately and publicly. What is the best place to do this?

    Ⓐ a web page
    Ⓑ the local newspaper
    Ⓒ the national newspaper
    Ⓓ a magazine

7. You are writing an article about the stresses involved in being a high school student and what to do about them. What is the best medium of publication?

    Ⓐ a magazine for teenagers
    Ⓑ a website aimed at teenagers
    Ⓒ a national newspaper
    Ⓓ both A and B

8. What is the best place to search for a specific recipe you need in a hurry?

    Circle the correct answer choice.

    Ⓐ Internet
    Ⓑ magazine
    Ⓒ newspaper
    Ⓓ recipe books

6 Ways to Become a Wake Board Whiz

1. Relax and be Patient

Relaxing on the board helps you get a better center of gravity, which keeps you stable on the board. The more loose and relaxed you are, the better balance you will have. Bend your knees, stay low to the board, keep your arms straight and let the boat pull you. Focus on staying balanced first, you can try the fancy tricks when you get more comfortable on the board.

2. Know Which Foot Goes First

Once you're up on the board, figure out which foot you want to be forward. The two ways you can position your feet are "regular" and "goofy". The "regular" position is when the left foot is forward on the board and "goofy" is when the right foot leads. Don't let the names of the positions sway you to choose a certain way, both stances are totally normal, just choose to lead with whichever foot is more comfortable and feels natural.

3. Control your Board

Once you are totally comfortable standing on the board, you can practice controlling the board. Controlling the board allows you to decide which way you are going and lays the foundation for future, more complicated, tricks. To control the board, you want to lean away from the boat, shift your weight to your heels, and "carve" through the water by transferring your weight to your toes and back again.

4. Practice on Land

Thankfully, there are many ways to practice your wakeboard skills during the colder seasons that don't involve getting into freezing water. While on land, you can practice different balance exercises, like yoga, or you could invest in a balance board. A balance board is a board with a wheel in the middle that can be used indoors. To use it, you put your foot on either side of the board and try to stay stable to improve your balance. Once you get better at balance, you can also try doing tricks on

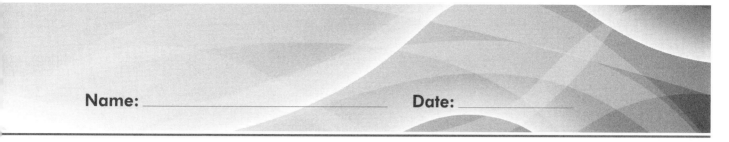
your balance board. This type of board improves your balance and strengthens your ankles, which will help you significantly once it's time to get back in the water. You can also practice on land through skateboarding or snowboarding. Both use similar muscles and can help you practice your balance, which lets you practice your skills on the off season.

5.   Lift More Weights

You might not think that lifting weights and getting stronger would help your wakeboarding skills, but it does. Wakeboarding uses so many muscles that you don't even think about- Biceps, abdominals, back, legs, forearms, etc. It truly is a sport that exercises the whole body, which is why it is important to strength train. Having strong muscles helps your balance on the board, your ability to do tricks, and allows you to get better faster than someone who does not weight train. Strength training also helps prevent injuries, as the stronger you are, the easier it will be to ride with correct form.

6.   Try some Tricks

Once you have the basics down, you can start practicing tricks. One of the most basic tricks is an Ollie. An ollie is simply a jump that you do while on the board. To do an ollie, get up on the board and begin riding. Once you feel comfortable on the board, shift your weight to your back leg and lift your front leg quickly, pushing off from the water from the back of the board. Once you're in the air, bring your back leg up to the same level as your front leg to level the board. When landing, try to keep the board flat, putting equal pressure on both of your feet. This keeps your board from braking and you from falling off. Once you perfect the ollie, you can start doing more complicated tricks.

Week 4 Online Activity

Login to the Lumos student account and complete the following activities.

1. Reading assignment
2. Vocabulary practice
3. Write your summer diary

If you haven't created your Lumos account, use the URL and access code below to get started.
URL: http://www.lumoslearning.com/a/tedbooks
Access Code: G8-9MLSLH-73851

Week 5 Summer Practice

Transformations of Parallel Lines (8.G.A.1.C)

Day 1

1. Two parallel line segments move from Quadrant One to Quadrant Four. Their slopes do not change. What transformation has taken place?

   Ⓐ Reflection
   Ⓑ Translation
   Ⓒ Dilation
   Ⓓ This is not a transformation.

2. Two parallel line segments move from Quadrant One to Quadrant Four. Their slopes change from a positive slope to a negative slope. What transformation has taken place?

   Ⓐ Reflection
   Ⓑ Rotation
   Ⓒ Translation
   Ⓓ It could be either a rotation or a reflection.

3. Two parallel line segments move from Quadrant One to Quadrant Two. Their slopes change from a negative slope to a positive slope. What transformation has taken place?

   Ⓐ Reflection
   Ⓑ Rotation
   Ⓒ Translation
   Ⓓ It could be either a rotation or a reflection.

4. **Select what concepts are preserved under these different transformations. Select all that apply.**

	Lengths of sides	Angle Measures	Parallel Sides on Figure
Translation	☐	☐	☐
Reflection	☐	☐	☐
Rotation	☐	☐	☐
Dilation	☐	☐	☐

Evaluating Authors Claims (RI.8.8)

Day 1

5. What is an author's claim?

- (A) his or her argument
- (B) the support for his or her argument
- (C) his or her opinion
- (D) the facts for the argument

6. What evidence must you look at in evaluating an author's claim?

- (A) the argument itself
- (B) the support that the author provides to back up his or her argument
- (C) the author's opinion about that which he or she is arguing
- (D) how many people support the argument.

7. What is the best way to determine the accuracy of evidence provided by the author?

- (A) ask somebody
- (B) personal experience
- (C) look it up on the computer, any site will do
- (D) do your own research

8. Determine whether the following statement is a fact, supported opinion, or unsupported opinion:

Texas is the hottest state in the United States.

Write your answer in the box given below.

Transformations of Congruency (8.G.A.2)

Day 2

1. **Which of the following examples best represents congruency in nature?**

    Ⓐ A mother bear and her cub.
    Ⓑ The wings of a butterfly.
    Ⓒ The tomatoes picked from my garden.
    Ⓓ The clouds in the sky.

2. **If triangle ABC is drawn on a coordinate plane and then reflected over the vertical axis, which of the following statements is true?**

    Ⓐ The reflected triangle will be similar ONLY to the original.
    Ⓑ The reflected triangle will be congruent to the original.
    Ⓒ The reflected triangle will be larger than the original.
    Ⓓ The reflected triangle will be smaller than the original.

3. **What transformation was applied to the object in quadrant 2 to render the results in the graph below?**

    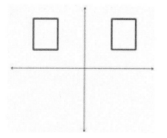

    Ⓐ reflection
    Ⓑ rotation
    Ⓒ translation
    Ⓓ not enough information

4. Quadrilateral ABCD is translated 5 units to the left and 4 units down. Which congruent quadrilateral match this transformation?

Write your answer in the box given below

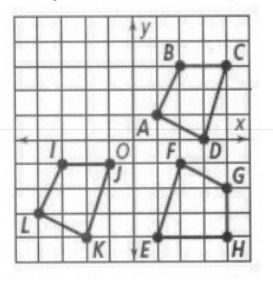

Day 2

5. **When you come across two conflicting viewpoints, what should you do?**

   Ⓐ research other sources to find out which fact is correct
   Ⓑ look to see if the fact may have changed
   Ⓒ examine the reliability of both writers
   Ⓓ all of the above

6. **Determine whether the writers are presenting conflicting information based on fact or interpretation.**

   Writer One: Geology is a branch of science.
   Writer Two: Geology is a branch of math.

   Ⓐ fact
   Ⓑ opinion

7. **Determine whether the writers are presenting conflicting information based on fact or interpretation.**

   Writer One: The president's sweater was too small.
   Writer Two: The president's sweater fit him well.

   Ⓐ fact
   Ⓑ opinion

8. **Determine whether the following is fact or opinion.**

   Bailey is wearing blue shoes.

   Write your answer in the box given below.

Day 3

1. **Which of the following transformations could transform triangle A to triangle B?**

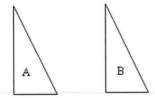

Ⓐ Rotation
Ⓑ Reflection
Ⓒ Translation
Ⓓ Dilation

2. **Which of the following transformations could transform triangle A to triangle B?**

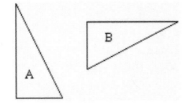

Ⓐ Rotation
Ⓑ Reflection
Ⓒ Translation
Ⓓ Dilation

3. **Which of the following transformations could transform triangle A to triangle B?**

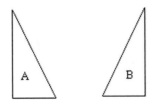

Ⓐ Rotation
Ⓑ Reflection
Ⓒ Translation
Ⓓ Dilation

4. Select the coordinates that will correspond with each transformation for point A.

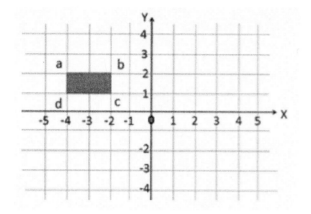

	A(4, -2)	A(-2, 1)	A(-4, -2)
Translation (x+2, y-1)	○	○	○
Rotation 180°	○	○	○
Reflection over x-axis	○	○	○

Adjectives and Adverbs (L.8.1.A)

Day 3

5. What is an adjective?

- Ⓐ a word that modifies (describes) a verb
- Ⓑ a word that modifies (describes) a noun in a sentence
- Ⓒ a word that modifies (describes) a sentence
- Ⓓ a word that modifies (describes) descriptive words

6. What is an adverb?

- Ⓐ a word that modifies (describes) adjectives
- Ⓑ a word that modifies (describes) verbs
- Ⓒ a word that modifies (describes) adverbs
- Ⓓ a word that modifies (describes) descriptive words

7. A lot of people have trouble with the words "good" and "well". See if you can use them correctly in the following sentences by choosing the correct the words in correct sequence.

a) I am _____.
b) Dinner was really _____ .
c) They are _____ baseball players.
d) You play really_____.

- Ⓐ well, well, good, good
- Ⓑ well, good, well, good
- Ⓒ well, good, good, good
- Ⓓ well, good, good, well

8. What is the adjective in the following sentence?

Greg bounced around the playground, happily playing on his new slide.

Write your answer in the box given below.

_____

Day 4

1. Which of the following transformations could transform triangle A to triangle B?

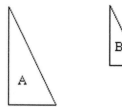

Ⓐ Rotation
Ⓑ Reflection
Ⓒ Translation
Ⓓ Dilation

2. What transformations have been applied to the large object to render the results in the graph below?

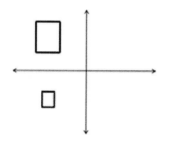

Ⓐ reflection and dilation
Ⓑ rotation and translation
Ⓒ translation and dilation
Ⓓ None of the above

3. What transformations have been applied to the large object to render the results in the graph below?

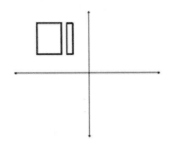

   Ⓐ no transformation
   Ⓑ reflection and dilation
   Ⓒ translation and dilation
   Ⓓ rotation and dilation

4. Select which transformations were used to map the pre-image onto the image. Also select if the transformation used leaves the figure congruent or if it only makes them similar.

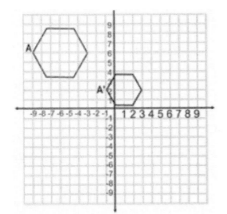

	Used	Similar only	Congruent
Translation	○	○	○
Rotation	○	○	○
Reflection	○	○	○
Dilation	○	○	○

Day 4

5. Select the correct verb form to agree with the subject in the following sentence.

Either the teacher or the principal _____ going to contact you.

Ⓐ are
Ⓑ is
Ⓒ not
Ⓓ never

6. Which sentence shows the correct subject-verb agreement?

a) Neither the cat nor the dogs have been fed.
b) Neither the cat nor the dogs has been fed.

Ⓐ a
Ⓑ b

7. Select the correct verb form to agree with the subject in the following sentence.

_____ my sister or my parents going to pick me up?

Ⓐ Is
Ⓑ Are
Ⓒ you're
Ⓓ watching

8. Fill in the blank with the correct verb.

The boys and girls _____ very excited about the trip next week.

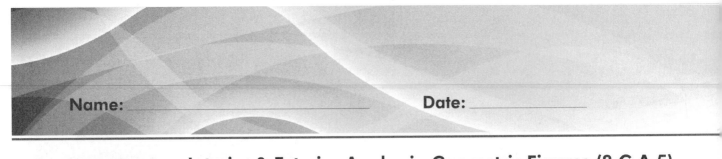

Name: _____ Date: _____

Day 5

Interior & Exterior Angles in Geometric Figures (8.G.A.5)

1. What term describes a pair of angles formed by the intersection of two straight lines that share a common vertex but do not share any common sides?

Ⓐ Supplementary Angles
Ⓑ Complementary Angles
Ⓒ Horizontal Angles
Ⓓ Vertical Angles

2. If a triangle has two angles with measures that add up to 100 degrees, what must the measure of the third angle be?

Ⓐ 180 degrees
Ⓑ 100 degrees
Ⓒ 80 degrees
Ⓓ 45 degrees

3.

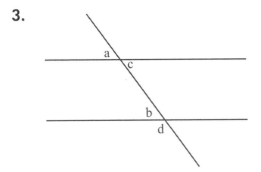

The figure shows two parallel lines intersected by a third line. If a = 55°, what is the value of b?

Ⓐ 35°
Ⓑ 45°
Ⓒ 55°
Ⓓ 125°

4. **Match the figure with the sum of the interior angles of each polygon.**

	2520	1080	1440	4140	540
Decagon	○	○	○	○	○
16-gon	○	○	○	○	○
Pentagon	○	○	○	○	○
25-gon	○	○	○	○	○
Octagon	○	○	○	○	○

Pronouns (L.8.1.C)

Day 5

5. Select the pronoun that will best fit into the following sentence.

The instructor put _____ students at ease when he said no one would fail.

- Ⓐ we
- Ⓑ his
- Ⓒ their
- Ⓓ them

6. Select the pronoun that will best fit into the following sentence.

My grandmother and _____ enjoyed spending the day together at the fair.

- Ⓐ I
- Ⓑ myself
- Ⓒ me
- Ⓓ my

7. Select the pronoun that will best fit into the following sentence.

_____ students laughed so loudly that the class next door was distracted from their lesson.

- Ⓐ They
- Ⓑ Us
- Ⓒ Them
- Ⓓ Those

8. Fill in the blank with the correct pronoun:

Julie couldn't believe _____ friend didn't listen to _____ advice.

Maze Game

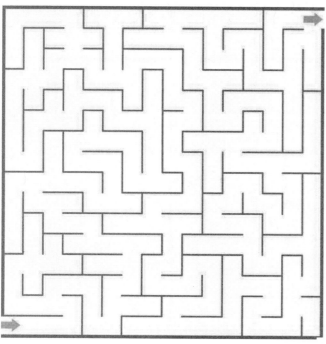

Help the beautiful kite fly out of the maze.

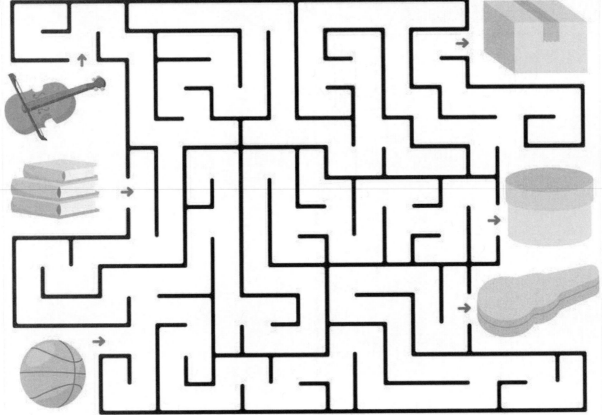

Week 5 Online Activity

Login to the Lumos student account and complete the following activities.

1. Reading assignment
2. Vocabulary practice
3. Write your summer diary

If you haven't created your Lumos account, use the URL and access code below to get started.

URL: http://www.lumoslearning.com/a/tedbooks

Access Code: G8-9MLSLH-73851

Week 6 Summer Practice

Day 1

Verifying the Pythagorean Theorem (8.G.B.6)

1. Which of the following could be the lengths of the sides of a right triangle?

   Ⓐ 1, 2, 3
   Ⓑ 2, 3, 4
   Ⓒ 3, 4, 5
   Ⓓ 4, 5, 6

2. A triangle has sides 8 cm long and 15 cm long, with a 90° angle between them. What is the length of the third side?

   Ⓐ 7 cm
   Ⓑ 17 cm
   Ⓒ 23 cm
   Ⓓ 289 cm

3. Find the value of c, rounded to the nearest tenth.

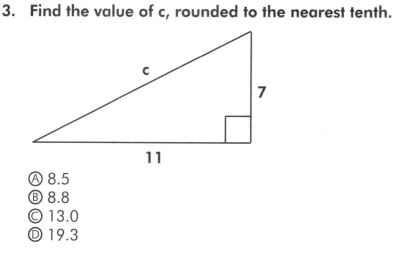

   Ⓐ 8.5
   Ⓑ 8.8
   Ⓒ 13.0
   Ⓓ 19.3

4. Which equation would you use to solve for the missing side of the triangle pictured below?

Circle the correct answer choice.

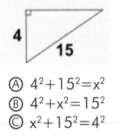

   Ⓐ $4^2+15^2=x^2$
   Ⓑ $4^2+x^2=15^2$
   Ⓒ $x^2+15^2=4^2$

Phrases and Clauses (L.8.1.C)

Day 1

5. Which of the following sentences is an infinitive phrase?

Ⓐ To make my birthday special, my family threw me a surprise party.
Ⓑ My teacher, the one wearing the blue dress, gave us our final yesterday.
Ⓒ Mary waited at the bus stop, hoping another would come by.
Ⓓ On the side of the road, we saw a perfectly good couch.

6. Identify whether the following is an independent or subordinate clause.

The boy cried.

7. Identify whether the following is an independent or subordinate clause.

When I jumped down

Ⓐ independent
Ⓑ subordinate

8. Is the clause in the following sentence independent or subordinate?

My son, an accomplished fisherman, caught the largest fish in the tournament.

Pythagorean Theorem in Real-World Problems (8.G.B.7)

Day 2

1. The bottom of a 17-foot ladder is placed on level ground 8 feet from the side of a house as shown in the figure below. Find the vertical height at which the top of the ladder touches the side of the house.

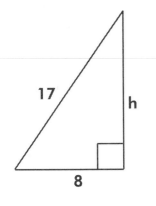

Ⓐ h = 9 feet
Ⓑ h = 12 feet
Ⓒ h = 15 feet
Ⓓ h = 18 feet

2. Which of the following equations could be used to find the value of w?

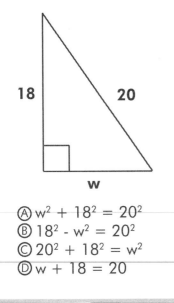

Ⓐ $w^2 + 18^2 = 20^2$
Ⓑ $18^2 - w^2 = 20^2$
Ⓒ $20^2 + 18^2 = w^2$
Ⓓ $w + 18 = 20$

3. John has a chest where he keeps his antiques. What is the measure of the diagonal (d) of John's chest with the height (c) = 3ft, width (b) = 3ft, and length (a) = 5ft.?

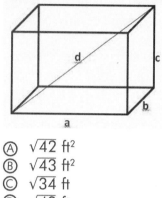

Ⓐ $\sqrt{42}$ ft²
Ⓑ $\sqrt{43}$ ft²
Ⓒ $\sqrt{34}$ ft
Ⓓ $\sqrt{43}$ ft

4. Match the following word problem with the correct equation that you would use to solve it.

	$9^2+x^2=15^2$	$40^2+38^2=x^2$	$9^2+15^2=x^2$	$x^2+38^2=40^2$
One house is 15 miles due north of the park. Another house is 9 miles due east of the park. How far apart are the houses from each other?	◯	◯	◯	◯
The foot of a ladder is put 9 feet from the wall. If the ladder is 15 feet long how high up the building will the ladder reach?	◯	◯	◯	◯
If you drive your car 40 miles south and then 38 miles east, how far would the shortest route be from your starting point?	◯	◯	◯	◯
The diagonal of a TV is 40 inches. The TV is 38 inches long. How tall is the TV?	◯	◯	◯	◯

Day 2

5. What is the definition of a verbal?

- Ⓐ a spoken form of communication
- Ⓑ forms of verbs that function as other parts of speech
- Ⓒ a very descriptive word
- Ⓓ a word that contains a sound

6. Which verbals function as adjectives?

- Ⓐ infinitives
- Ⓑ participles
- Ⓒ gerunds
- Ⓓ nouns

7. Which verbals function as nouns?

- Ⓐ infinitives
- Ⓑ gerunds
- Ⓒ participles
- Ⓓ verbs

8. What part of speech is the verbal taking in the following sentence?

Jogging is my least favorite cardio activity.

Circle the correct answer choice.

- Ⓐ noun
- Ⓑ adjective
- Ⓒ adverbial

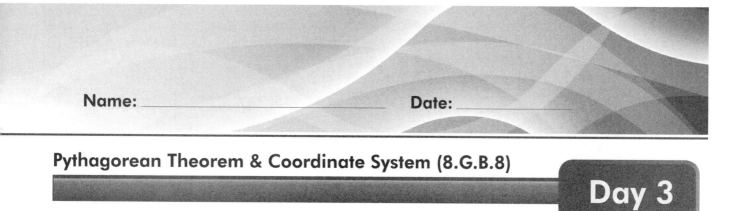

Pythagorean Theorem & Coordinate System (8.G.B.8)

Day 3

1. A robot begins at point A, travels 4 meters west, then turns and travels 7 meters south, reaching point B. What is the approximate straight-line distance between points A and B?

   Ⓐ 8 meters
   Ⓑ 9 meters
   Ⓒ 10 meters
   Ⓓ 11 meters

2. What is the distance between the points (1, 3) and (9, 9)?

   Ⓐ 6 units
   Ⓑ 8 units
   Ⓒ 10 units
   Ⓓ 12 units

3. Find the distance approximately between Pt A (2, 7) and Pt B (-2, -7).

   Ⓐ 14.0
   Ⓑ 14.6
   Ⓒ 18.0
   Ⓓ 13.4

4. Match the ordered pairs with the approximate distance between them.

	10.8	12.2	13	14.8
(6, 5) and (-4, 9)	○	○	○	○
(-8, 0) and (5, -7)	○	○	○	○
(-4, -9) and (6, -2)	○	○	○	○
(5, 4) and (12, 15)	○	○	○	○

Day 3

5. What comes first in active voice?

- Ⓐ subject
- Ⓑ object
- Ⓒ action
- Ⓓ fall

6. What is passive voice?

- Ⓐ when the writer uses a very nice tone of voice
- Ⓑ when the writer says nice things
- Ⓒ a sentence that is not a question or command
- Ⓓ a sentence in which the subject is acted upon instead of doing the action

7. What is active voice?

- Ⓐ when somebody talks a lot
- Ⓑ a sentence with a lot of action
- Ⓒ a sentence in which the subject is performing the action
- Ⓓ when someone talks and performs an activity at the same time

8. Identify whether the following sentence is written in the active or passive voice.

Much to her mother's dismay, Chloe colored on the dining room table.

Write your answer in the box given below.

Day 4

1. What is the volume of a sphere with a radius of 6?

    Ⓐ 72π
    Ⓑ 144π
    Ⓒ 216π
    Ⓓ 288π

2. A cone has a height of 9 and a base whose radius is 4. Find the volume of the cone.

    Ⓐ 18 π
    Ⓑ 36 π
    Ⓒ 48 π
    Ⓓ 72 π

3. What is the volume of a cylinder with a radius of 5 and a height of 3?

    Ⓐ 30
    Ⓑ 45
    Ⓒ 75
    Ⓓ 120

4. Find the volume of the figure below. Use pi = 3.14. Write your answer in the box below.

    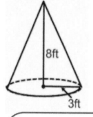
    8ft
    3ft

Punctuation (L.8.2.A)

Day 4

5. **Determine which sentence shows the correct usage of the comma.**

    Ⓐ Please pick up glue, scissors, and construction paper.
    Ⓑ The names of my pets are, Max, Goldie, and Emily.
    Ⓒ I looked everywhere for my keys, including the trash and under the couch and in the kitchen.
    Ⓓ My father Jim and my mother Martha enjoy camping dancing and jogging together.

6. **The following sentence is missing one or more commas. Determine which example shows the correct comma placement.**

    Ⓐ My uncle, who is an incredibly talented actor encouraged me to try out in the talent show.
    Ⓑ My uncle who is an incredibly talented actor, encouraged me to try out in the talent show.
    Ⓒ My uncle, who is an incredibly talented actor, encouraged me to try out for the talent show.
    Ⓓ My uncle who, is an incredibly talented actor, encouraged me to try out for the talent show.

7. **How would you fix the following sentence?**

    After you have finished taking out the trash you may watch your favorite show.

    Ⓐ After you have finished, taking out the trash you may watch your favorite show.
    Ⓑ After you have finished taking out the trash, you may watch your favorite show.
    Ⓒ After, you have finished taking out the trash you may watch your favorite show.
    Ⓓ After you have finished taking out the trash you may watch your favorite show.

8. **What is the best way to fix the following sentence?**

    Yvettes invitation for Brendas surprise party said to bring the following things to the party cupcakes soda and a gag gift

Day 5

1. If a scatter plot has a line of best fit that decreases from left to right, which of the following terms describes the association?

   Ⓐ Positive association
   Ⓑ Negative association
   Ⓒ Constant association
   Ⓓ Nonlinear association

2. If a scatter plot has a line of best fit that increases from left to right, which of the following terms describes the association?

   Ⓐ Positive association
   Ⓑ Negative association
   Ⓒ Constant association
   Ⓓ Nonlinear association

3. Following is 10 days of data which shows the sale of apples and mangoes. Fill in the type of association there is between the apple and mango sales.

DAYS	1	2	3	4	5	6	7	8	9	10
APPLE	62	49	81	26	45	55	16	74	97	34
MANGO	36	44	49	37	26	11	76	83	64	81

There is [   ] between apple and mango sale

4. Which of the following scatter plots is the best example of a linear association?

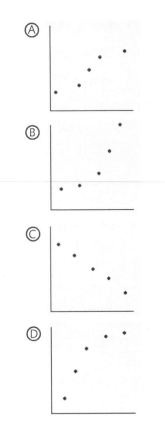

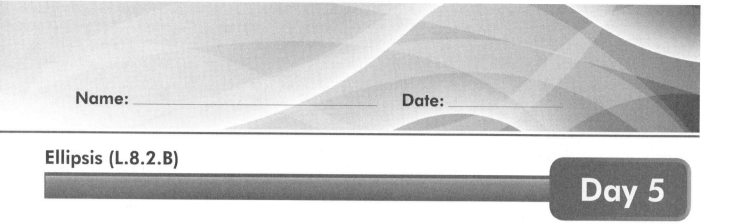

Ellipsis (L.8.2.B)

Day 5

5. Which of the following symbols is an ellipsis?

Ⓐ ...
Ⓑ ;
Ⓒ :
Ⓓ --

6. What is the purpose of an ellipsis?

Ⓐ to indicate text has been omitted
Ⓑ to add extra significance to a sentences
Ⓒ to end sentence powerfully
Ⓓ Both A and B

7. An ellipsis can be used to create suspense.

Ⓐ True
Ⓑ False

8. When is it appropriate to use an ellipsis? Circle the correct answer choice.

Ⓐ when citing evidence from a text that is long
Ⓑ when researching and information is at the beginning and end of a paragraph
Ⓒ when trying to be concise and only use necessary facts
Ⓓ all of the above

Summer Learning Activity Videos

Use the link below or QR code to watch the videos

http://lumoslearning.com/a/summervideos

Beating the Summer Academic Loss

Beating the Brain Drain through Literacy

Beating the Brain Drain through Computing

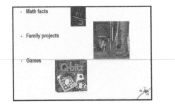

Warm-Up to a Great School Year

Week 6 Online Activity

Login to the Lumos student account and complete the following activities.

1. Reading assignment
2. Vocabulary practice
3. Write your summer diary

If you haven't created your Lumos account, use the URL and access code below to get started.

URL: http://www.lumoslearning.com/a/tedbooks

Access Code: G8-9MLSLH-73851

Week 7 Summer Practice

Scatter Plots, Line of Best Fit (8.SP.A.2)

Day 1

1.

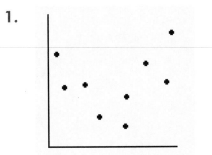

Which of the following best describes the points in this scatter plot?

Ⓐ Increasing Linear
Ⓑ Decreasing Linear
Ⓒ Constant Linear
Ⓓ None of these

2.

Which of the following best describes the points in this scatter plot?

Ⓐ Increasing Linear
Ⓑ Decreasing Linear.
Ⓒ Constant Linear
Ⓓ None of these

3.

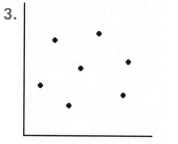

Which of the following lines best approximates the data in the scatter plot shown above?

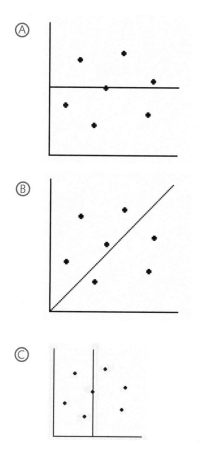

(A)

(B)

(C)

(D) None of these; the data do not appear to be related linearly.

4. Write the prediction equation for this graph using the two labeled points. Leave as fractions.

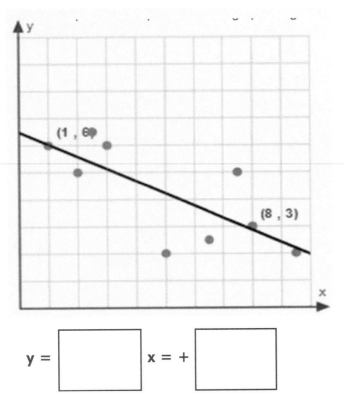

y = [   ]   x = + [   ]

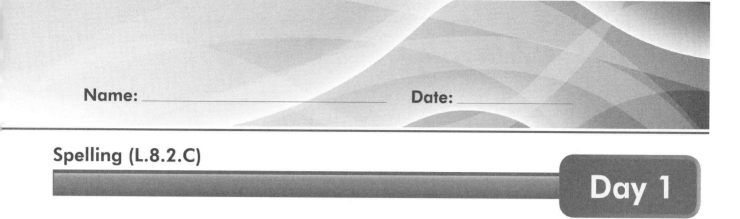

Spelling (L.8.2.C)

Day 1

5. What are homophones or homonyms?

- Ⓐ the scientific name for humans
- Ⓑ two or more words that are pronounced the same but have different meanings
- Ⓒ two or more words that mean the opposite
- Ⓓ none of the above

6. Choose the words that correctly complete the following sentence. Make sure that you pick the answer that shows the words in the correct sequence, as they would appear in the sentence.

I accidentally _____ the ball _____ the living room window.

- Ⓐ through/ threw
- Ⓑ threw/ though
- Ⓒ threw/ through
- Ⓓ through/through

7. Choose the words that correctly complete the following sentence. Make sure that you pick the answer that shows the words in the correct sequence, as they would appear in the sentence.

My cousins are so silly. _____ always running late because _____ are no alarm clocks in _____ house to wake them up in the morning.

- Ⓐ There, they're, their
- Ⓑ They're, there, their
- Ⓒ Their, there, they're
- Ⓓ There, there, there

8. What is the correct spelling for the misspelled word in the sentence below?

I am going to perswade my mother to buy me a dog.

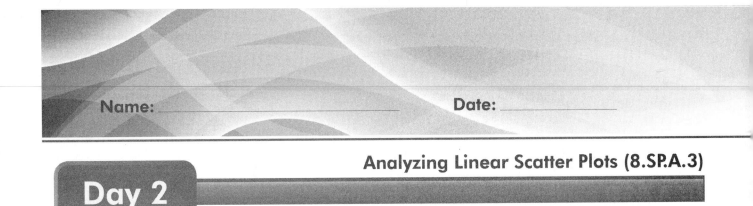

Analyzing Linear Scatter Plots (8.SP.A.3)

Day 2

1.

Which of the following scatter plots below demonstrates the same type of data correlation as the one shown above?

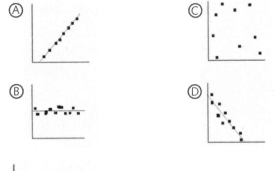

2.

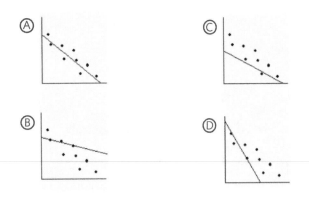

Which of the following lines most accurately models the points in this scatter plot?

3.

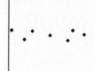

Which of the following lines most accurately models the points in this scatter plot?

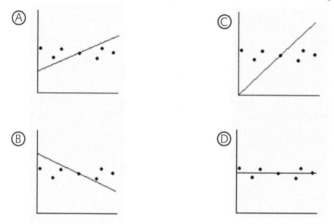

4. Match the correct vocab term with the correct definition.

	Linear	Negative Association	Line of Best Fit	Prediction Equation
A line on a graph showing the general direction that a group of points seem to be heading	○	○	○	○
A graph that is represented by a straight line	○	○	○	○
The equation of a line that can predict outcomes using given data	○	○	○	○
A correlation of points that is linear with a negative slope	○	○	○	○

Day 2

5. All verbs in the English language have which of the following?

- Ⓐ mood
- Ⓑ tense
- Ⓒ voice
- Ⓓ all of the above

6. What of the following is NOT a mood in verbs?

- Ⓐ active
- Ⓑ subjunctive
- Ⓒ indicative
- Ⓓ imperative

7. In which of the following instances would the subjunctive mood be necessary?

- Ⓐ writing about a hypothetical situation
- Ⓑ making a wish
- Ⓒ making a suggestion
- Ⓓ all of the above

8. Which of the following sentences is written in the indicative mood?

Circle the correct answer choice.

- Ⓐ It will rain tomorrow.
- Ⓑ It might rain tomorrow.
- Ⓒ Prepare for the rain tomorrow.
- Ⓓ none of the above

Day 3

1. 50 people were asked whether they were wearing jeans and whether they were wearing sneakers. The results are shown in the table below.
    What percent of the people who wore sneakers were also wearing jeans?

	Jeans	No Jeans
Sneakers	15	10
No Sneakers	5	20

    Ⓐ 15%
    Ⓑ 30%
    Ⓒ 60%
    Ⓓ 75%

2. 50 people were asked whether they were wearing jeans and whether they were wearing sneakers. The results are shown in the table below.
    What percent of the people who wore jeans were also wearing sneakers?

	Jeans	No Jeans
Sneakers	15	10
No Sneakers	5	20

    Ⓐ 15%
    Ⓑ 30%
    Ⓒ 60%
    Ⓓ 75%

3. 50 people were asked whether they were wearing jeans and whether they were wearing sneakers. The results are shown in the table below.
    What percent of the people who did NOT wear sneakers were wearing jeans?

	Jeans	No Jeans
Sneakers	15	10
No Sneakers	5	20

    Ⓐ 5%
    Ⓑ 20%
    Ⓒ 25%
    Ⓓ 40%

4. Using the data from the table below match the answers to the questions about the table. June surveyed the 7th and 8th grades to see which class they liked better, math or English. The results are shown in the two-way table below.

	Math	English
7th grade	78	67
8th grade	86	45

	131	.60	145	.66
Total number of 7th graders surveyed	○	○	○	○
Total number of 8th graders surveyed	○	○	○	○
The relative frequency of 7th grade students that chose English to all students that chose English	○	○	○	○
The relative frequency of 8th grader students that chose Math to the total number of 8th graders	○	○	○	○

Context Clues (L.8.4.A)

Day 3

5. The context of a word means _____.

- Ⓐ the words that surround it
- Ⓑ words that don't mean the same as they say
- Ⓒ using detail
- Ⓓ finding facts to support

6. What should you do when using context clues?

- Ⓐ Read the sentence containing the unfamiliar word, leaving that word out.
- Ⓑ Look closely at the words around the unfamiliar word to help guess its meaning.
- Ⓒ Substitute a possible meaning for the word and read the sentence to see if it makes sense.
- Ⓓ all of the above

7. Brian appeared infallible on the basketball court because he never missed a shot.

What is the best meaning of infallible?

- Ⓐ incapable of making an error
- Ⓑ imperfect
- Ⓒ faulty
- Ⓓ unsure of what he's doing

8. What is the best definition of foreboding?

Circle the correct answer choice.

- Ⓐ good fortune
- Ⓑ bad feeling
- Ⓒ fortune
- Ⓓ anticipation

Day 4

Rational vs. Irrational Numbers (8.NS.A.1)

1. Complete the following statement: Pi is _____ .

   Ⓐ both real and rational
   Ⓑ real but not rational
   Ⓒ rational but not real
   Ⓓ neither real nor rational

2. Complete the following statement: $\sqrt{7}$ is _____.

   Ⓐ both a real and a rational number
   Ⓑ a real number, but not rational
   Ⓒ a rational number, but not a real number
   Ⓓ neither a real nor a rational number

3. The number 57 belongs to which of the following set(s) of numbers?

   Ⓐ N only
   Ⓑ N, W, and Z only
   Ⓒ N, W, Z, and Q only
   Ⓓ All of the following: N, W, Z, Q, and R

4. Identify the irrational number and circle it.

   Ⓐ $\dfrac{5}{7}$
   Ⓑ 0.1
   Ⓒ $\sqrt{10}$

Day 4

5. What is a homonym?

Ⓐ words that sound the same but have different meanings and spellings
Ⓑ words that sound the same and have the same spelling but different meaning
Ⓒ words that do not sound the same or have the same spelling or meaning
Ⓓ words that neither sound or look alike

6. What is the correct definition of a homophone?

Ⓐ words that sound and look alike
Ⓑ words that sound alike but are spelled differently
Ⓒ words that sound different but mean the same thing
Ⓓ none of the above

7. Which meaning of the word "address" is used in the following sentence?

One should always address the president as, "Mr. President".

Ⓐ a formal communication
Ⓑ a place where a person or organization can be contacted
Ⓒ to direct a speech
Ⓓ the place you live

8. Which are the synonyms of graduation. More than one answer maybe correct. Select all the correct ones.

Ⓐ completion
Ⓑ confidence
Ⓒ realize
Ⓓ concentration
Ⓔ culmination
Ⓕ close

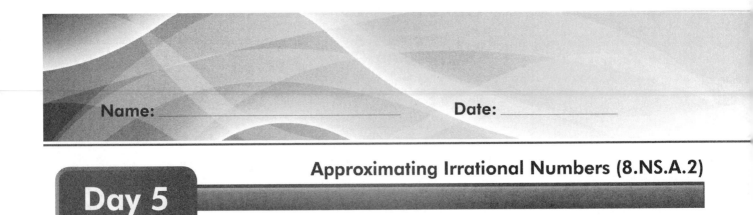

Approximating Irrational Numbers (8.NS.A.2)

Day 5

1. Which of the following numbers has the least value?

   Ⓐ $\sqrt{(0.6561)}$
   Ⓑ 0.8
   Ⓒ 0.8...
   Ⓓ 0.8884

2. Choose the correct order (least to greatest) for the following real numbers.

   Ⓐ $\sqrt{5}$, $4\frac{1}{2}$, 4.75, $2\sqrt{10}$

   Ⓑ $4\frac{1}{2}$, $\sqrt{5}$, $2\sqrt{10}$, 4.75

   Ⓒ $4\frac{1}{2}$, 4.75, $\sqrt{5}$, $2\sqrt{10}$

   Ⓓ $\sqrt{5}$, $2\sqrt{10}$, $4\frac{1}{2}$, 4.75

3. Which of the following numbers has the greatest value?

   Ⓐ 0.4...
   Ⓑ 0.444
   Ⓒ $\sqrt{0.4}$
   Ⓓ 0.45

4. Which is the correct order of the following numbers when numbering from least to greatest?

   Ⓐ $\sqrt{0.9}$, 0.9, 0.999, 0.9...
   Ⓑ 0.9, $\sqrt{0.9}$, 0.999, 0.9...
   Ⓒ 0.9, 0.9..., $\sqrt{0.9}$, 0.999
   Ⓓ 0.9, 0.9..., 0.999, $\sqrt{0.9}$

Roots, Affixes, and Syllables (L.8.4.B)

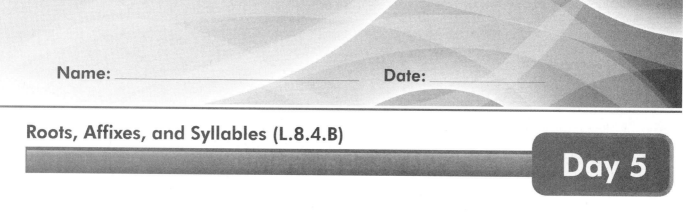

Day 5

5. Where does the prefix go in a word?

Ⓐ at the end
Ⓑ at the beginning
Ⓒ in the middle
Ⓓ none of the above

6. Where does a suffix go in a word?

Ⓐ at the end
Ⓑ at the beginning
Ⓒ in the middle
Ⓓ none of the above

7. What is an affix?

Ⓐ a repair for something
Ⓑ a prefix or suffix attached to a root to form a new word
Ⓒ a sound made by blends of letters
Ⓓ the phonetic understanding of words

8. The suffix "er" means a person who does an action. What does "announcer" mean?

Circle the correct answer choice.

Ⓐ someone who announces
Ⓑ someone who works on automobiles
Ⓒ someone who works for a news station
Ⓓ all of the above

Word Puzzles

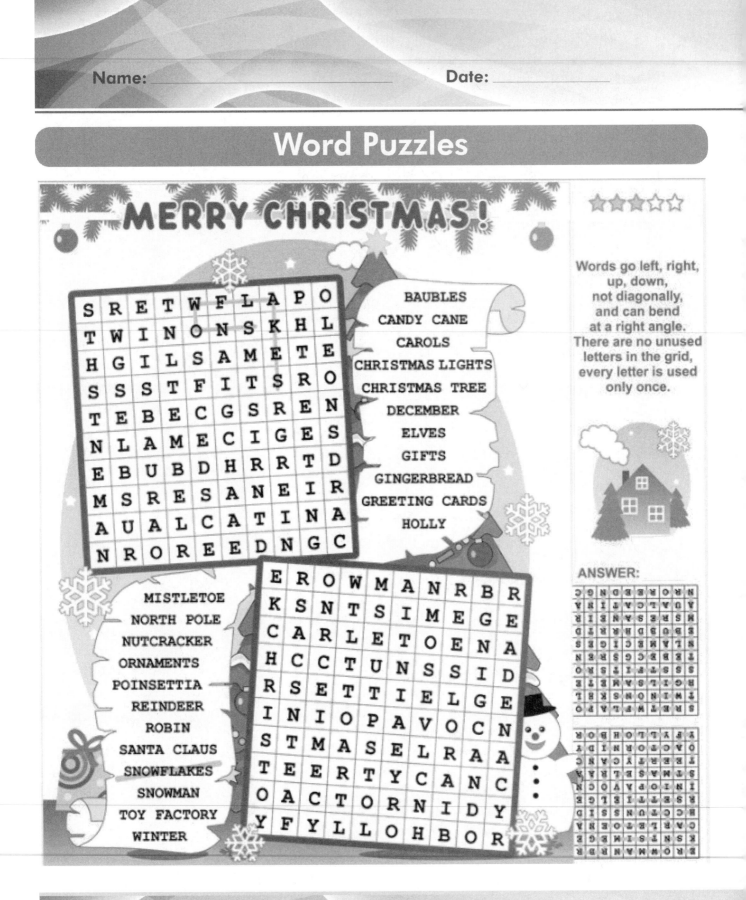

MERRY CHRISTMAS!

S	R	E	T	W	F	L	A	P	O
T	W	I	N	O	N	S	K	H	L
H	G	I	L	S	A	M	E	T	E
S	S	S	T	F	I	T	S	R	O
T	E	B	E	C	G	S	R	E	N
N	L	A	M	E	C	I	G	E	S
E	B	U	B	D	H	R	R	T	D
M	S	R	E	S	A	N	E	I	R
A	U	A	L	C	A	T	I	N	A
N	R	O	R	E	E	D	N	G	C

BAUBLES
CANDY CANE
CAROLS
CHRISTMAS LIGHTS
CHRISTMAS TREE
DECEMBER
ELVES
GIFTS
GINGERBREAD
GREETING CARDS
HOLLY

Words go left, right,
up, down,
not diagonally,
and can bend
at a right angle.
There are no unused
letters in the grid,
every letter is used
only once.

MISTLETOE
NORTH POLE
NUTCRACKER
ORNAMENTS
POINSETTIA
REINDEER
ROBIN
SANTA CLAUS
SNOWFLAKES
SNOWMAN
TOY FACTORY
WINTER

E	R	O	W	M	A	N	R	B	R
K	S	N	T	S	I	M	E	G	E
C	A	R	L	E	T	O	E	N	A
H	C	C	T	U	N	S	S	I	D
R	S	E	T	T	I	E	L	G	E
I	N	I	O	P	A	V	O	C	N
S	T	M	A	S	E	L	R	A	A
T	E	E	R	T	Y	C	A	N	C
O	A	C	T	O	R	N	I	D	Y
Y	F	Y	L	L	O	H	B	O	R

ANSWER:

UNDERWATER WORLD

★★★☆☆

Words go left, right, up, down, not diagonally, and can bend at a right angle. There are no unused letters in the grid, every letter is used only once.

Grid 1:

S	S	H	A	S	H	C	R	A	B
T	I	S	R	K	E	L	L	N	A
G	N	E	A	H	O	D	O	C	E
R	A	Y	L	O	R	O	L	P	H
S	Q	U	S	B	S	H	W	H	I
T	D	I	T	O	E	S	L	A	N
U	R	T	E	C	F	I	E	L	R
J	E	L	R	T	O	P	U	A	E
E	S	E	A	B	E	D	S	R	E
L	L	Y	F	I	S	H	C	O	F

Word List 1:
ANEMONE
COD
CORAL REEF
CRAB
DOLPHIN
FISH
FLYING FISH
HALIBUT
HERRING
JELLYFISH
LOBSTER
MORAY EEL
MUSSEL
OCEAN
OCTOPUS

Word List 2:
OYSTER
PLANKTON
SALMON
SCUBA DIVING
SEABED
SEAHORSE
SEAWEED
SHARK
SHELL
SQUID
STARFISH
STINGRAY
TURTLE
URCHIN
WHALE

Grid 2:

S	A	L	M	A	N	E	M	E	T
S	M	O	O	P	N	K	O	N	U
T	A	R	N	L	A	T	O	N	B
S	R	A	Y	U	R	M	L	E	I
C	F	I	E	E	C	U	S	S	L
U	B	S	H	L	H	I	N	H	A
C	A	D	I	V	O	T	E	R	D
O	D	G	N	I	Y	S	G	S	E
F	I	N	H	S	E	H	N	E	E
L	Y	G	F	I	R	R	I	A	W

ANSWER:

Name: _____ Date: _____

Week 7 Online Activity

Login to the Lumos student account and complete the following activities.

1. Reading assignment
2. Vocabulary practice
3. Write your summer diary

If you haven't created your Lumos account, use the URL and access code below to get started.

URL: http://www.lumoslearning.com/a/tedbooks

Access Code: G8-9MLSLH-73851

Week 8 Summer Practice

Day 1

1. Which of the following is equivalent to $X^{(2-5)}$?

   (A) X^3

   (B) $X^{\frac{1}{3}}$

   (C) $\dfrac{1}{X^3}$

   (D) 3^X

2. $1^9 =$

   (A) 1
   (B) 3
   (C) 9
   (D) $\dfrac{1}{9}$

3. $(X^{-3})(X^{-3}) =$

   (A) X^6
   (B) X^9
   (C) $\dfrac{1}{X^6}$
   (D) $\dfrac{1}{X^9}$

4. Simplify this expression and write your answer in the box below
   $a^7(a^8)(a)$

Reference Materials (L.8.4.C)

Day 1

5. **Which of the following are acceptable reference materials to use for a research assignment?**

   Ⓐ questionnaires
   Ⓑ experiments
   Ⓒ field studies
   Ⓓ scholarly articles
   Ⓔ all of the above

6. **How can you determine whether a source is reliable?**

   Ⓐ If you obtained your information from the Internet, it is always reliable.
   Ⓑ You should consider who wrote the source and why.
   Ⓒ If you obtained your information from an actual article, it will be reliable.
   Ⓓ answer choices B & C

7. **Why must you be very careful about obtaining information from websites?**

   Ⓐ It can be difficult to find reputable sources.
   Ⓑ Some sites can be edited by anyone.
   Ⓒ It is too easy to find what may look like good information but sources are often unverifiable.
   Ⓓ all of the above

8. **If you were researching Anne Frank, which of the following would be your choice for a primary source?**

   Circle the correct answer choice.

   Ⓐ your teacher
   Ⓑ an encyclopedia
   Ⓒ a website about Anne Frank
   Ⓓ Anne Frank's diary

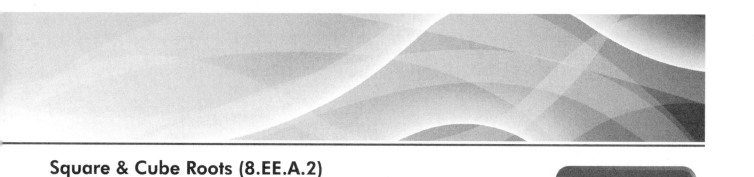

Square & Cube Roots (8.EE.A.2)

Day 2

1. The square root of 110 is between which two integers?

    (A) 10 and 11
    (B) 9 and 10
    (C) 11 and 12
    (D) 8 and 9

2. Solve the following problem: $6\sqrt{20} \div \sqrt{5} = $ _____

    (A) 12
    (B) 11
    (C) 30
    (D) 5

3. The cube root of 66 is between which two integers?

    (A) 4 and 5
    (B) 3 and 4
    (C) 5 and 6
    (D) 6 and 7

4. Select all the numbers which have integers as the cube roots.

    (A) $\sqrt[3]{27}$
    (B) $\sqrt[3]{9}$
    (C) $\sqrt[3]{1000}$
    (D) $\sqrt[3]{18}$

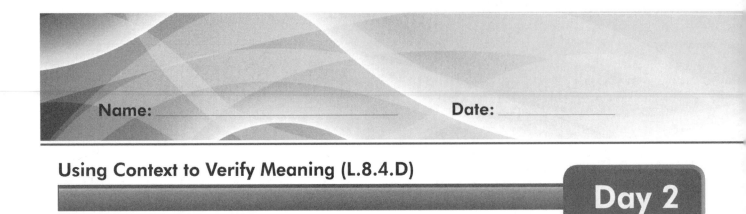

Using Context to Verify Meaning (L.8.4.D)

Day 2

Marathon

Training for a marathon takes hard work and **perseverance**. It is not something you can do on the **spur** of the moment. Preparing for a marathon takes months, particularly if you have never run a marathon before. The official distance of a full marathon is 26.2 miles. In 2005, the average time to complete a marathon in the United States was 4 hours 32 minutes 8 seconds for men and 5 hours 6 minutes 8 seconds for women.

Most people who run marathons are not trying to win. Many runners try to beat their own best time. Some compare their time to other runners in the same gender and age group. Some people set time-oriented goals, such as finishing under four hours, while others try to complete the race without slowing to a walk. Many beginners simply hope to finish the marathon.

Trainers recommend that beginners maintain a **consistent** running schedule for six weeks prior to even starting a marathon training program. The purpose of this is to allow the body to adapt to the **various** physical demands of long-distance running. First-time marathon runners should train by running four days a week for at least four months, increasing distance by no more than ten percent weekly. As race day approaches, runners should **taper** their runs, reducing the strain on their bodies and resting before the marathon. It is important not to **overexert** yourself during training because that can lead to a lot of injuries. Most common injuries are spraining of the knees and ankles. These sprains can **hinder** the training.

Before the race, it is important to stretch in order to keep muscles **limber**. Staying hydrated is also important, but there is a danger in drinking too much water. If a runner drinks too much water, they may experience a dangerous condition called **hyponatremia**, a drop of sodium levels in the blood. During the race, trainers recommend maintaining a steady pace. It is normal to feel sore after a marathon. Light exercise will help sore muscles heal faster.

Some people run marathons in pairs or groups. Training for and running a marathon with another person or group of people can make the experience more enjoyable and more rewarding. A running partner might be just the motivation you need to show up for an early morning run instead of rolling over to hit the snooze button. And, when you cross the finish line together, you can share the satisfaction of reaching your common goal.

Usually, thousands of people sign up and run a marathon. Most people finish the race. The thrill of running a marathon for the first time is unbelievable. The training sessions are harder if you have never run before. But it is unbelievable what ones' body can do when one puts his/her mind to it. Having a good coach to support you makes all the difference in training for a marathon.

The daily runs are very important. Strength training and core training are also very important.

The health benefits you gain from training are tremendous. Your core muscles grow stronger, and you will have tighter thighs and gluts. Your heart will be much stronger, and you can maintain lower cholesterol and blood sugar levels. Overall, you will look better and become healthier.

Nothing can explain how people feel when they reach that finish line at the end of the race. All the hard work and months of training feel worthwhile. The feeling of accomplishing something great overtakes you. It is great to run a marathon, but it is even greater to finish it.

Using context clues in the story determine the meaning of the bold words.

5. perseverance

Ⓐ determination
Ⓑ routine
Ⓒ flexibility
Ⓓ practice

6. spur

Ⓐ after long planning
Ⓑ without planning
Ⓒ with much discussion
Ⓓ with significant thought

7. consistent

Ⓐ varying
Ⓑ changing
Ⓒ regular
Ⓓ dynamic

8. "If you cannot determine a word's meaning in context, where can you look? From among the 4 choices given below, select the correct answer and enter it in the box given below."

Ⓐ thesaurus
Ⓑ dictionary
Ⓒ encyclopedia
Ⓓ journal

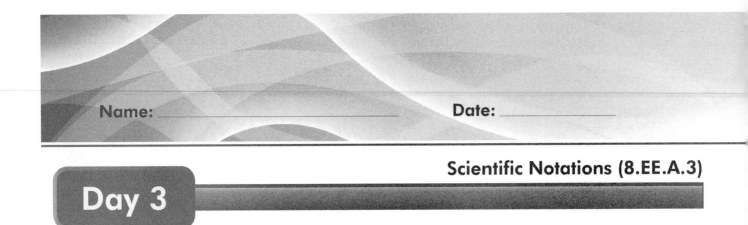
1. The approximate population of Kazakhstan is 1.53×10^7 people. Express this number in standard notation.

    Ⓐ 153,000
    Ⓑ 1,530,000
    Ⓒ 15,300,000
    Ⓓ 153,000,000

2. The typical human body contains about 2.5×10^{-3} kilograms of zinc. Express this amount in standard form.

    Ⓐ 0.00025 kilograms
    Ⓑ 0.0025 kilograms
    Ⓒ 0.025 kilograms
    Ⓓ 0.25 kilograms

3. If a number expressed in scientific notation is $N \times 10^5$, how large is the number?

    Ⓐ Between 1,000 (included) and 10,000
    Ⓑ Between 10,000 (included) and 100,000
    Ⓒ Between 100,000 (included) and 1,000,000
    Ⓓ Between 1,000,000 (included) and 10,000,000

4. Change 2,347,000,000 from standard form to scientific notation by filling in the blank boxes.

$\times 10$

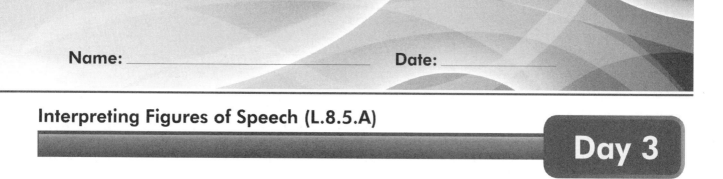
Interpreting Figures of Speech (L.8.5.A)

Day 3

5. How is a metaphor different than a simile?

- Ⓐ A metaphor is the same as a simile.
- Ⓑ A metaphor does not use like or as in the comparison of two unlike things.
- Ⓒ A metaphor is not at all similar to a simile.
- Ⓓ A metaphor uses like or as in the comparison of two unlike things.

6. What two figures of speech listed below have to do with word sounds?

- Ⓐ metaphor and simile
- Ⓑ personification and idiom
- Ⓒ alliteration and onomatopoeia
- Ⓓ noun and verb

7. Which of the following is a metaphor?

- Ⓐ It is as hot as the surface of the sun out there.
- Ⓑ She sold seashells by the seashore.
- Ⓒ I stayed up too late last night studying and now my mind is foggy.
- Ⓓ She plopped on the sofa after babysitting nine hours.

8. What figure of speech is used in the following sentence:

Sarah was like a toddler hungry for food; I was ready to get out of the car with her.

Write your answer in the box given below.

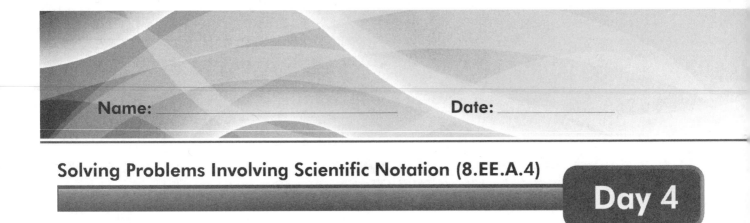
Solving Problems Involving Scientific Notation (8.EE.A.4)

Day 4

1. Simplify $(2 \times 10^{-3}) \times (3 \times 10^5)$ and express the result in scientific notation.

   Ⓐ 5×10^{-8}
   Ⓑ 5×10^{-15}
   Ⓒ 6×10^8
   Ⓓ 6×10^2

2. Washington is approximately 2.4×10^3 miles from Utah. Mary drives 6×10 miles per hour from Washington to Utah. Divide the distance by the speed to determine the approximate number of hours it takes Mary to travel from Washington to Utah.

   Ⓐ 41 hours
   Ⓑ 40 hours
   Ⓒ 39 hours
   Ⓓ 38 hours

3. Which of the following is NOT equal to $(5 \times 10^5) \times (9 \times 10^{-3})$?

   Ⓐ 4.5×10^4
   Ⓑ 4.5×10^3
   Ⓒ $4,500$
   Ⓓ 45×100

4. Which of the following is correctly ordered from greatest to least?

   Note that more than one option may be correct. Select all the correct answers.

   Ⓐ 2.0×10^2, 3.0×10^6, 4.0×10^{-7}, 5.0×10^{12}
   Ⓑ 4.0×10^{-7}, 2.0×10^2, 3.0×10^6, 5.0×10^{12}
   Ⓒ 3.0×10^7, 3.0×10^6, 3.0×10^2, 3.0×10^{-7}
   Ⓓ 1.8×10^9, 1.5×10^6, 1.4×10^{-5}, 1.9×10^{-8}

Day 4

5. What is an analogy?

Ⓐ words that mean the opposite
Ⓑ a comparison of two words
Ⓒ a short story
Ⓓ the study of ants

6. Select the best choice to explain the relationship of the words in the following analogy.

branch is to tree as fingers are to hand

Ⓐ antonyms
Ⓑ synonyms
Ⓒ part to whole
Ⓓ whole to part

7. Select the best choice to finish the following analogy.

repel is to attract as _____ is to lead

Ⓐ follow
Ⓑ guide
Ⓒ direct
Ⓓ head

8. Words that express extreme exaggeration are called as _____

Identify the figure of speech defined by above sentence.

Compare Proportions (8.EE.B.5)

Day 5

1. **Which of the following ramps has the steepest slope?**

    Ⓐ Ramp A has a vertical rise of 3 feet and a horizontal run of 15 feet
    Ⓑ Ramp B has a vertical rise of 4 feet and a horizontal run of 12 feet
    Ⓒ Ramp C has a vertical rise of 2 feet and a horizontal run of 10 feet
    Ⓓ Ramp D has a vertical rise of 5 feet and a horizontal run of 20 feet

2. **Choose the statement that is true about unit rate.**

    Ⓐ The unit rate can also be called the rate of change.
    Ⓑ The unit rate can also be called the mode.
    Ⓒ The unit rate can also be called the frequency.
    Ⓓ The unit rate can also be called the median.

3. **Which statement is false?**

    Ⓐ Unit cost is calculated by dividing the amount of items by the total cost.
    Ⓑ Unit cost is calculated by dividing the total cost by the amount of items.
    Ⓒ Unit cost is the cost of one unit item.
    Ⓓ On similar items, a higher unit cost is not the better price.

4. **Solve for the proportion for the missing number.**

    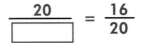

    $$\frac{20}{\boxed{}} = \frac{16}{20}$$

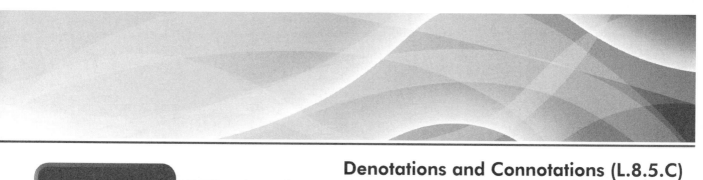

Day 5

5. **The denotation of a word is the literal dictionary definition. The connotation of a word is the idea or feeling associated with the word.**

   Is the underlined word used denotatively or connotatively?

   That girl is <u>immature</u> and impossible to be around because she is always goofing around and is a huge disruption in class.

   Ⓐ denotatively
   Ⓑ connotatively
   Ⓒ both

6. **Which of the following words has the most positive connotation?**

   dwelling, house, home, residence

   Ⓐ dwelling
   Ⓑ house
   Ⓒ home
   Ⓓ residence

7. **Which of the following words has the most negative connotation?**

   cheap, frugal, thrifty

   Ⓐ cheap
   Ⓑ frugal
   Ⓒ thrifty

8. **My mom screamed when she realized she won first place in the pie baking contest.**

   Does the word "screamed" in the above sentence have a positive, negative, or neutral connotation?

Online Review of High School

Login to your student account and explore High School Math and English Language Arts topics!

Math	ELA
• Number and Quantity - The Real Number System • Number and Quantity - Quantities • Number and Quantity - The Complex Number System • Number and Quantity - Vector & Matrix Quantities • Algebra - Seeing Structure in Expressions • Algebra - Arithmetic with Polynomials & Rational Expressions • Algebra - Creating Equations • Algebra - Reasoning with Equations & Inequalities • Functions - Interpreting Functions • Functions - Building Functions • Functions - Linear, Quadratic, & Exponential Models • Functions - Trigonometric Functions • Geometry - Congruence • Geometry - Similarity, Right Triangles, & Trigonometry • Geometry - Circles • Geometry - Expressing Geometric Properties with Equations • Geometry - Geometric Measurement & Dimension • Geometry - Modeling with Geometry • Statistics & Probability - Interpreting Categorical & Quantitative Data • Statistics & Probability - Making Inferences & Justifying Conclusions • Statistics & Probability - Conditional Probability & the Rules of Probability • Statistics & Probability - Using Probability to Make Decisions	• Reading: Literature • Reading: Informational Text • Writing • Speaking & Listening • Language

If you haven't created your Lumos account, use the URL and access code below to get started.

URL: http://www.lumoslearning.com/a/tedbooks
Access Code: G8-9MLSLH-73851

Hello Ron Miller!

Try our new chrome extension - Lumos WordUp: Vocabulary Practice ✖

| HIGH SCHOOL | GRADE 8 |

Your Study Programs:

HS
MATH

Lumos StepUp - High School Math Workbooks   0%

HS
ELA

Lumos StepUp - High School ELA Workbooks   0%

Week 8 Online Activity

Login to the Lumos student account and complete the following activities.

1. Reading assignment
2. Vocabulary practice
3. Write your summer diary

If you haven't created your Lumos account, use the URL and access code below to get started.
URL: http://www.lumoslearning.com/a/tedbooks
Access Code: G8-9MLSLH-73851

Week 9 Summer Practice

Understanding Slope (8.EE.B.6)

Day 1

1. Which of these lines has the greatest slope?

   Ⓐ $y = \frac{8}{5}x - 7$

   Ⓑ $y = \frac{6}{5}x + 4$

   Ⓒ $y = \frac{7}{5}x + 2$

   Ⓓ $y = \frac{9}{5}x - 3$

2. Which of these lines has the smallest slope?

   Ⓐ $y - \frac{1}{8}x + 7$

   Ⓑ $y - \frac{1}{3}x + 7$

   Ⓒ $y - \frac{1}{4}x - 9$

   Ⓓ $y = \frac{1}{7}x$

3. Fill in the blank with one of the four choices to make the following a true statement. Knowing _____ and the y-intercept is NOT enough for us to write equation of the line.

   Ⓐ direction
   Ⓑ a point on a given line
   Ⓒ the x-intercept
   Ⓓ the slope

4. Find the slope between the points (3, -3) and (12, -2).

Write your answer in the box given below.

Domain Specific Words (L.8.6)

Day 1

5. **What is jargon?**

   Ⓐ words that are silly
   Ⓑ words that are specific to an area a study
   Ⓒ words that are slang
   Ⓓ words that describe nouns

6. **Given the task to write an essay about literature, what would be a good domain specific vocabulary word to use?**

   Ⓐ plot
   Ⓑ characterization
   Ⓒ dialogue
   Ⓓ all of the above

7. **Read the sentence below; identify a domain specific vocabulary word in it.**

   After reading the novel, it is clear that the author's use of setting is meant a symbol for bravery.

   Ⓐ symbol
   Ⓑ bravery
   Ⓒ use
   Ⓓ author's

8. **What word in the following sentence is a domain specific vocabulary word?**

   The poem can be interpreted in many ways. Readers can begin their interpretation by looking at a poem's meter, and then by closely examining its rhyme scheme and its rhythm. The overall interpretation should include the many nuances of the poem.

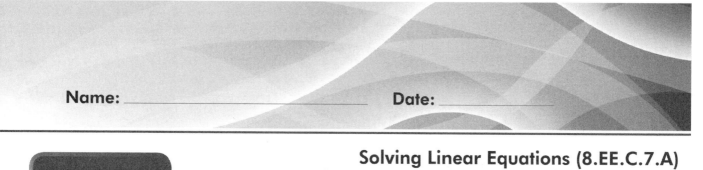

Day 2

1. Find the solution to the following equation: 3x + 5 = 29

   Ⓐ x = 24
   Ⓑ x = 11
   Ⓒ x = 8
   Ⓓ x = 6

2. Find the solution to the following equation:
   7 - 2x = 13 – 2x

   Ⓐ x = -10
   Ⓑ x = -3
   Ⓒ x = 3
   Ⓓ There is no solution.

3. Find the solution to the following equation: 6x + 1 = 4x - 3

   Ⓐ x = -1
   Ⓑ x = -2
   Ⓒ x = - 0.5
   Ⓓ There is no solution.

4. Solve for x: 5x + 20 = -20.

   x = ?

   Write your answer in the box given below.

Capitalization (L.8.2)

5. Which of the following words should always be capitalized?

(A) Grandmother
(B) the first word of every sentence
(C) names of subjects, such as Science
(D) all of the above

6. What is the correct way to capitalize "grandmother" in the below sentences?

a. We should go visit (grandmother/ Grandmother) today.
b. This weekend we went to see my (grandmother/ Grandmother).

(A) grandmother, grandmother
(B) Grandmother, grandmother
(C) grandmother, Grandmother
(D) None of the above

7. Which words need to be capitalized in the following sentences?

next week, my report on wwll is due. I have an awful lot of studying and research to complete; it looks like I will spending a lot of time at the Joann Darcy public library.

(A) next
(B) wwll
(C) public library
(D) all of the above

8. Which word should be capitalized in the following sentence?

Betty and I are going to france for spring break.

Write your answer in the box given below.

Day 3

Solve Linear Equations with Rational Numbers (8.EE.C.7.B)

1. $4x + 2(x - 3) = 0$

   Ⓐ $x = 0$
   Ⓑ $x = 1$
   Ⓒ $x = 2$
   Ⓓ All real values for x are correct solutions.

2. **Solve the following equation for y.**
   $3y - 7(y + 5) = y - 35$

   Ⓐ $y = 0$
   Ⓑ $y = 1$
   Ⓒ $y = 2$
   Ⓓ All real values for y are correct solutions.

3. **Solve the following linear equation:** $2(x-5) = \frac{1}{2}(6x+4)$

   Ⓐ $x = -12$
   Ⓑ $x = -9$
   Ⓒ $x = -4$
   Ⓓ There is no solution.

4. **Solve the following linear equation:**

   $$\frac{8}{16} = n + \frac{8}{16}n$$

Textual Evidence (RL.8.1)

Day 3

Sympathy

I lay in sorrow, deep distressed;
My grief a proud man heard;
His looks were cold, he gave me gold,
But not a kindly word.

My sorrow passed-I paid him back
The gold he gave to me;
Then stood erect and spoke my thanks
And blessed his charity.
I lay in want, and grief, and pain;
A poor man passed my way;
He bound my head, He gave me bread,
He watched me day and night.

How shall I pay him back again
For all he did to me ?
Oh, gold is great, but greater far
Is heavenly sympathy.
-       Charles Mackay

5. Which line in the poem tells you that the poet is grateful to the poor man?

Ⓐ   How shall I pay him back again, for all he did to me?
Ⓑ   I lay in want, in grief and pain;
Ⓒ   His looks were cold, he gave me gold. But not a kindly word.
Ⓓ   Then stood erect and spoke my thanks, and blessed his charity.

6. How did the proud man treat the poet when he lay in sorrow and deep distress?

Ⓐ   in an affectionate way
Ⓑ   in an aloof, unsympathetic manner
Ⓒ   with a lot of concern
Ⓓ   with respect and kindness

The Mountain and The Squirrel	The Arrow and the Song
The mountain and the squirrel Had a quarrel; And the former called the latter, "Little Prig." Bun replied "You are doubtless very big; But all sorts of things and weather Must be taken in together To make up a year And a sphere. And I think it no disgrace To occupy my place. If I'm not so large as you, Your are not so small as I, And not half so spry; I'll not deny you make A very pretty squirrel track; Talents differ; all is well and wisely put; If I cannot carry forests on my back, Neither can you crack a nut" Ralph Waldo Emerson (1803 - 1882)	I shot an arrow into the air It fell to earth, I knew not where; For, so swiftly it flew, the sight Could not follow it in its flight. I breathed a song into the air It fell to earth, I knew not where For who has sight so keen and strong That it can follow the flight of song? Long, long afterward, in an oak I found the arrow, still unbroke And the song, from beginning to end I found again in the heart of a friend. H. W. Longfellow (1807 - 1882)

7. **Which line in "The Mountain and the Squirrel" told the reader that the squirrel recognizes everyone has a different talent?**

   Ⓐ Talents differ; all is well and wisely put;
   Ⓑ You are doubtless very big;
   Ⓒ And I think it no disgrace
      To occupy my place.
   Ⓓ I'll not deny you make
      A very pretty squirrel track;

Patrick couldn't believe it. The most important day of his life so far; the day he had been waiting for had finally arrived! He was so excited to show the coaches how hard he had been working on his pitching. He just knew he would make the team this year. Looking at the clock, Patrick realized he was running late. "Bye, Mom," he yelled as he scrambled out of the house. Backing down the driveway, he saw his mom run out of the house, and it looked like she was trying to get his attention. He didn't have time to wait, so he drove off.

Although the school was only five minutes away, the drive felt like an eternity. Two red lights later, Patrick screeched into the parking lot, slammed the car into park, and ran around to the trunk to get his bat bag. It wasn't there. Every piece of equipment he needed to prove himself to the coaches this year was in that bag.

8. Part A

What was Patrick's mom likely trying to tell Patrick?

Ⓐ "Don't drive too fast!"
Ⓑ "Don't be late for tryouts!"
Ⓒ "Be careful driving!"
Ⓓ He forgot his bat bag!

8. Part B

The reader can tell from the story that Patrick _____.

Ⓐ had tried out for the team before and not made it.
Ⓑ was a fast runner.
Ⓒ was not at all ready for tryouts.
Ⓓ was not excited to tryout for the team.

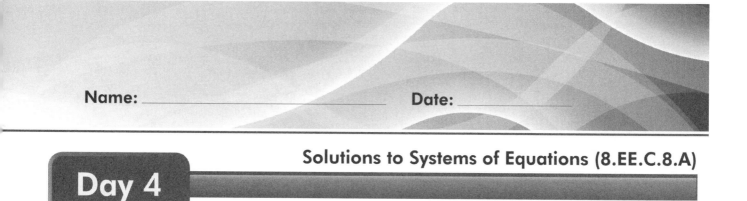
Solutions to Systems of Equations (8.EE.C.8.A)

Day 4

1. Use the graph, to find the solution to the following system:

$$\frac{x}{2} + \frac{y}{3} = 2$$

$$3x - 2y = 48$$

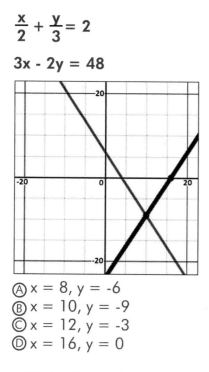

Ⓐ x = 8, y = -6
Ⓑ x = 10, y = -9
Ⓒ x = 12, y = -3
Ⓓ x = 16, y = 0

2. Which of the following best describes the relationship between the graphs of the equations in this system?
   y = 2x - 6
   y = -2x + 6

   Ⓐ The lines intersect at the point (0, -3).
   Ⓑ The lines intersect at the point (3, 0).
   Ⓒ The lines do not intersect because their slopes are opposites and their y-intercepts are opposites.
   Ⓓ They are the same line because their slopes are opposites and their y-intercepts are opposites.

3. Solve the system:

   2x + 3y = 14
   2x - 3y = -10

   Ⓐ x = 1, y = 4
   Ⓑ x = 2, y = 12
   Ⓒ x = 4, y = 2
   Ⓓ x = 10, y = 10

4. Anya is three years older than her brother, Cole. In 11 years, Cole will be twice Anya's current age. Find their current ages.

   Circle the correct answer choice.

   Ⓐ Anya: 11 years old, Cole: 8 years old
   Ⓑ Anya: 10 years old, Cole: 7 years old
   Ⓒ Anya: 9 years old, Cole: 6 years old
   Ⓓ Anya: 8 years old, Cole: 5 years old

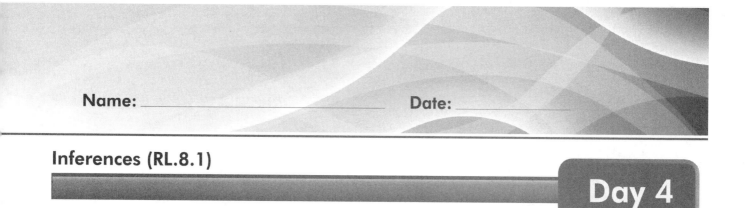

Inferences (RL.8.1)

Day 4

When Samantha saw the new boy in class, her heart started pounding so fast and loudly that she was certain everybody could hear it. She straightened her posture and gently swept her bangs behind her right ear. As the boy sat down next to her, she gave him a quick glance and then a friendly smile. She was sure he noticed her bright red cheeks as she bent over her paper.

5. Which of the following can be inferred about Samantha based on the above passage?

   Ⓐ She thought the boy had a nice backpack.
   Ⓑ She was scared of the boy.
   Ⓒ She thought the boy was cute.
   Ⓓ She thought the boy was mean.

Maya and her family were headed to the beach one sunny summer afternoon. When they arrived, Maya noticed a family seemed to be having what appeared to be a garage sale, which was a curious sight to see in the beach parking lot. They were selling used personal items that you would normally find in one's house like pots, pans, dishes, a CD player, and various other items. There appeared to be a mother, father, and two children, a boy and a girl about Maya's age. Maya could tell that the family was not there to enjoy the beach as they were not dressed for the beach. Their clothes were far too warm for the beautiful day and were tattered, torn, and quite dingy. Suddenly, Maya remembered that she had a twenty dollar bill in her pocket that she had received for her birthday.

6. Based on the information in the passage, infer what you think will happen next.

   Ⓐ Maya will buy something from the family's garage sale.
   Ⓑ Maya will want to buy something, but she already has all of those items in her house, so she won't buy anything.
   Ⓒ Maya will give the money to her family.
   Ⓓ Maya will use the money for snacks for the family.

Henry sat eagerly in the waiting area of the airport. Over the last year, he'd been putting away a little money each month into what he called his "vacation fund." He bought travel books and researched all of the sites he wanted to see. Now all he had to do was wait until his flight was called.

7. What can you infer about Henry's trip?

Ⓐ It was a spur of the moment idea.
Ⓑ It is something he has looked forward to for a long time.
Ⓒ It is to a place he's been before.
Ⓓ It is to an exotic location.

She pulled hard at the doorknob. The door was difficult to budge. Finally inside, she brushed aside the cobwebs, leaving footprints in the dust on the floor.

8. What can be inferred from this description?

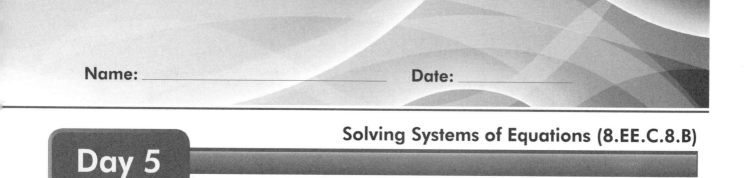

Day 5

1. **Solve the system:**
    x = 13 + 2y
    x - 2y = 13

    Ⓐ x = 0, y = 13
    Ⓑ x = 13, y = 0
    Ⓒ There is no solution.
    Ⓓ There are infinitely many solutions.

2. **Solve the system:**
    2x + 5y = 12
    2x + 5y = 9

    Ⓐ x = 1, y = 2
    Ⓑ x = 2, y = 1
    Ⓒ There is no solution.
    Ⓓ There are infinitely many solutions.

3. **Solve the system:**
    -4x + 7y = 26
    4x + 7y = 2

    Ⓐ x = -3, y = 2
    Ⓑ x = 3, y = -2
    Ⓒ x = -2, y = 3
    Ⓓ x = 2, y = -3

4. Select the systems that have no solution.

    Note that more than one option may be correct. Select all the correct answers.

    Ⓐ $y= -4x+7$
       $y=-3x+3$

    Ⓑ $y=\dfrac{3}{4}x-3$
       $y=\dfrac{3}{4}x+2$

    Ⓒ $y= x-2$
       $y=x+2$

    Ⓓ $y=2x+3$
       $4x-2y=8$

    Ⓔ $y+2x=-12$
       $y=x+15$

Theme (RL.8.2)

Day 5

5. What is the best way to find a theme in a story?

Ⓐ look at the first sentence of the story.
Ⓑ look at the names of the characters in a story.
Ⓒ look at the details in the story to find a larger meaning.
Ⓓ look at reviews of the story.

6. What is an implied theme?

Ⓐ a theme that is straightforward and requires no guessing
Ⓑ a theme that is indirectly stated through characters, plot, and setting of a story
Ⓒ a theme that is common throughout many stories that are told across many different cultures
Ⓓ a theme that is clearly stated by the main character in the story

The Fox and the Crow
Aesop's Fable

A Fox once saw a Crow fly off with a piece of cheese in its beak and settle on a branch of a tree. "That's for me, as I am a Fox," said Master Reynard, and he walked up to the foot of the tree. "Good-day, Mistress Crow," he cried. "How well you are looking today: how glossy your feathers; how bright your eye. I feel sure your voice must surpass that of other birds, just as your figure does; let me hear but one song from you that I may greet you as the Queen of Birds." The Crow lifted up her head and began to caw her best, but the moment she opened her mouth, the piece of cheese fell to the ground, only to be snapped up by Master Fox. "That will do," said he. "That was all I wanted. In exchange for your cheese, I will give you a piece of advice for the future."

7. What is the theme of this story?

Ⓐ Help out your friends.
Ⓑ Don't trust flatterers.
Ⓒ Sometimes, a song is necessary.
Ⓓ You should never have to work for food.

The Ungrateful Son
by Jacob and Wilhelm Grimm

Once, a man was sitting with his wife before their front door. They had a roasted chicken, which they were about to eat together. Then the man saw that his aged father was approaching, and he hastily took the chicken and hid it, for he did not want to share it with him. The old man came, had a drink, and went away. Now the son wanted to put the roasted chicken back onto the table, but when he reached for it, it had turned into a large toad, which jumped into his face and sat there and never went away again. If anyone tried to remove it, it looked venomously at him as though it would jump into his face, so that no one dared to touch it. And the ungrateful son was forced to feed the toad every day, or else it would eat from his face. And thus, he went to and fro in the world without rest.

8. Part A
What is the theme of this story?

A) The theme of the story is to always share what you have to share.
B) The theme of the story is to not be afraid of toads because they can keep you from saving someone's life.
C) The theme of the story is that you should always feed yourself first, and then you will be strong enough to help others.
D) The theme of the story is that you should always share your chicken with your parents.

8. Part B
The theme of The Ungrateful Son is implied because _____.

A) It is indirectly stated, and the reader has to determine the theme through the actions of the characters.
B) It is explicitly stated and the reader does not have to guess at all.
C) It is obvious and doesn't require much thought.
D) none of the above

Week 9 Online Activity

Login to the Lumos student account and complete the following activities.

1. Reading assignment
2. Vocabulary practice
3. Write your summer diary

If you haven't created your Lumos account, use the URL and access code below to get started.

URL: http://www.lumoslearning.com/a/tedbooks

Access Code: G8-9MLSLH-73851

Week 10

Lumos Short Story Competition 2020

Write a short story based on your summer experiences and get a chance to win $100 cash prize + 1 year free subscription to Lumos StepUp + trophy with a certificate.
To enter the competition follow the instructions.

Step 1

Visit **www.lumoslearning.com/a/tedbooks**
and enter your access code to create Lumos parent and student account.
Access Code : G8-9MLSLH-73851

Step 2

After registration, your child can upload their summer story by logging into the student portal and clicking on **Lumos Short Story Competition 2020.**

Note: *If you have already registered this book and using online resources need not register again. Students can simply log in to the student portal and submit their story for the competition.*
Visit: www.lumoslearning.com/a/slh2020 for more information

Last date for submission is August 31, 2020

Use the space provided below for scratch work before uploading your summer story Scratch Work

Answer Key &
Detailed Explanations

Week 1

Question No.	Answer	Detailed Explanation
1	A	An integer belongs to the set containing the counting numbers, their additive inverses, and zero. Therefore, (-3) is an integer.
2	B	Rational numbers are the set of numbers that can be expressed as the quotient of two integers in which the denominator is not zero. All whole numbers can be expressed in this manner; so every whole number is a rational number.
3	B	$\sqrt{10}$ cannot be expressed as the ratio of two integers p and q and is therefore irrational.
4	A, C	Rational numbers are numbers that can be expressed as a fraction. Since 5/7 is already a fraction that is one. The second answer, the square root of 25 gives you a whole number 5. This can be written as a fraction, 5/1. Thus, both are rational numbers.
5	C	Answer choice C is correct. Lines 3 and 4 in the third stanza provide the text evidence. There is no text evidence supporting answer choices A, B or D.
6	C	Answer choice C is correct and directly stated in the last two lines of the poem. Answer choice D is incorrect. While the poet does recognize gold is good, he states sympathy is greater. Answer choices A and B do not provide evidence to support the question.
7	A	Answer choice A is correct because the first line of the poem indicates the poet's sorrow. The other answer choices are incorrect as there is no evidence in the first stanza to support them.
8.A	D	Answer choice D is correct because all of the answers are supported by evidence from the text.
8.B	B	Answer choice B is correct as it states and describes the cabin in Innisfree. Answer choices A, C and D are incorrect as they do not provide evidence of a cabin in Innisfree.

Day 2

Question No.	Answer	Detailed Explanation
1	B	$2^2=4$ and $3^2=9$ Since 5 lies between 4 and 9, $\sqrt{5}$ lies between 2 & 3.
2	C	$(2.2)^2=4.84$ and $(2.3)^2=5.29$ Since 5 lies between 4.84 and 5.29 on the number line, $\sqrt{5}$ lies between 2.2 and 2.3.
3	C	If we change the numbers all to the same accuracy, it is easier to order them on the number line. Write 1.8 as 1.80, 2.5 as 2.50 and $\sqrt{5}$ as >2 because $2^2=4$ and < 2.5 because $2.5^2=6.25$. Then, the correct order is 1.35, 1.8, $\sqrt{5}$, 2.5.
4	C	$2.63^2 \approx 6.92$ $2.65^2 \approx 7.02$ The square root of 7 is about 2.64, so $\sqrt{7}$ falls between 2.63 and 2.65. Then, 2.5, 2.63, $\sqrt{7}$, 2.65 is the correct answer.
5	C	Answer choice C is correct. The poet, Yeats, is describing Innisfree as very peaceful and tranquil. All the descriptions that he uses indicate peace and tranquility. Answer choices A and B are incorrect because they are too specific. Each of them is contributes to the overall peace and tranquility.
6	A	Answer choice A is correct. The poet is thinking about where he will retire and fondly thinks about Innisfree as he walks to or from work. Answer choices B, C and D cannot be supported by the text.
7	B	Answer choice B is correct. Elizabeth was going to drive to work but could not because she did not have her keys. She locked them in the house. Answer choices A and C are not supported in the text.
8	C	Answer choice C is correct. When Mary covers her head and ears, this shows the reader she is frightened and trying to hide from the storm. Answer choices A, B, and D cannot be supported by the text.

Week 1

Question No.	Answer	Detailed Explanation
1	D	Unless there are parentheses to denote otherwise, the exponent is only applied to the constant or variable immediately preceding it. If there are parentheses immediately preceding it, then it is applied to everything within the parentheses.
2	D	When dividing quantities with like bases, you must subtract the exponents. $6 - (-2) = 8$ $$\frac{X^6}{X^{-2}} = X^{6-(-2)} = X^8$$
3	A	A quick way to change exponents from negative to positive is to move the expression to which the negative exponent is applied from the denominator to the numerator or vice versa and change the sign of the exponent. 3^{-2} is the same as $\frac{1}{3^2}$ which is the same as $\frac{1}{9}$.
4	B, C & D	The first example is using the Power of a Power Property $(4^2)^3 = 4^6$ because $4^2 \times 4^2 \, 4^2 = 4^{2+2+2} = 4^6$. The second one is Division Property of Exponents $8^5/8^1 = 8^4$. This is true because $$\frac{8 \times 8 \times 8 \times 8 \times 8}{8}$$ when simplified, leaves you with $8 \times 8 \times 8 \times 8$ which is 8^4. The last example is the Multiplicative Property of Exponents. $7^4 \times 7^4 = 7^8$ because $7 \times 7 \times 7 \times 7 \times 7 \times 7 \times 7 \times 7 = 7^8$
5	A	Answer choice A is correct. The theme of a piece is the underlying message of a piece of literature, and the main idea is a statement that tells what the piece is about. Answer choices B, C and D are incorrect and unreasonable.

Question No.	Answer	Detailed Explanation
6	C	Answer choice C is correct. A universal theme is one that can be found in many stories and pieces of literature and can be applied to any situation, any person or any era. It does not include character names. Answer choices A and D are incorrect. Neither answer is reasonable. Answer choice B is incorrect as the universal theme is not always implicit (not clearly stated). It is sometimes explicit (clearly stated).
7	A	Answer choice A is correct. The theme is always a statement as opposed to a one word description. Answer choices B, C, and D are incorrect.
8	A	Answer choice A is correct. Charlie learned that he should have listened to his mom when she was giving him instructions on doing the laundry. In this example, the reader thinks about what Charlie learned and then restates the lesson so that it applies universally - pay close attention when you are learning something new. This applies to both Charlie and the world (universal). Answer choices B, C, and D are not themes of this story.

Question No.	Answer	Detailed Explanation
1	A	$10^3 = 1,000$, So, the cube root of 1,000 is 10.
2	C	$8\sqrt{12} = 8\sqrt{(4 \times 3)} = 8(2)\sqrt{3} = 16\sqrt{3}$ $\sqrt{15} = \sqrt{(5 \times 3)}$ So $8\sqrt{12} \div \sqrt{15} = 16\sqrt{3} \div \sqrt{5}\sqrt{3}$
3	A	$8^2 = 64$ and $9^2 = 81$ Therefore, the square root of 75 is between 8 and 9.
4	$\sqrt[3]{8}=2$ since $2 \times 2 \times 2 = 8$	Taking the cube root of a number is finding a number that multiplied by itself 3 times will give you the number under the radical. In this case the cuberoot of 8 will equal 2 because $2 \times 2 \times 2 = 8$.
5	B	Answer choice B is correct. An objective summary is one that does not include an opinion. Answer choices A, C, and D are not definitions of an objective summary.
6	B	Answer choice B is correct. Objective summaries should always be brief, accurate, and objective. Additionally, they should not include details from the text. Answer choices A, C, and D do not describe the attributes of a good objective summary.
7	B	Answer choice B is correct. An objective summary should adequately summarize the text. Answer choice A is incorrect because an objective summary should not include opinions. Answer choice C is incorrect because a summary should not include information about all the characters in a text. Answer choice D is incorrect because a summary does not have a specific length.
8	-	During the summer, the ants stowed food so they would not go hungry during the winter. The grasshopper spent his summer playing music, so when winter came, he had nothing to eat.

Week 1

Question No.	Answer	Detailed Explanation
1	B	Moving the decimal in 3,380,000 just to the right of the first non-zero digit requires us to move it 6 places to the left resulting in 3.38×10^6.
2	C	If I move the decimal from standard notation to the right of the first non-zero digit, I must move it 8 places to the left. Therefore, 890,800,000 expressed in scientific notation is, 8.908×10^8.
3	B	Moving the decimal to the right 6 places from 3.8×10^6, we get 3,800,000.
4	C and D	Both the options (C) and (D) are correct because their first number is a decimal that is greater than 1 but less than 10. They are then multiplied by a power of 10. One is multiplied by a positive power of 10, making it a large number and the second one is multiplied by a negative power making it a really small number. Both are in correct form.
5	C	Answer choice C is correct. There are five elements of a plot. They are the introduction (sometimes identified as the exposition), rising action, climax, falling action, and resolution. Answer choices A, B, and D are incorrect.
6	A	Answer choice A is correct. The two types of conflict are internal and external. Internal conflict is when the struggle is between the character and himself. External conflict is when an outside force causes the conflict. Answer choices B, C, and D are incorrect.
7	B	Answer choice B is correct. The plot of the story is the series of events in the story. Answer choices A, C, and D are incorrect.
8.A	A	Answer choice A is correct. The conflict is that there is not enough money for a graduation party. This conflict is man vs fate because the students had not direct control. There are other conflicts in the story, but the major conflict is the lack of money. Answer choices B, C, and D are incorrect.
8.B	A	Answer choice A is correct. The conflict in the story is that there is not enough money for 8th grade graduation party. It is worth noting that the reader learns of the conflict in the introduction of the story. Answer choices B, C, and D are incorrect.

Question No.	Answer	Detailed Explanation
1	B	3.7×10^7 people $\div$ 1.6×10^5 square miles $=($ $3.7 \div 1.6)$ $\times$ 10^{7-5} $=$ 2.3125 $\times$ 10^2 people/square mile $=$ 231.25 people/sq. mi. 240 is the best estimate.
2	C	6×10^7 kilometers $\div$ 3×10^5 kilometers per second $=$ $(6 \div 3)$ $\times$ $10^{(7-5)}$ $=$ 2 $\times$ 10^2(kilometers $\div$ kilometers/ seconds) $=$ 2×10^2 seconds $=$ 200 seconds
3	A	$(4 \times 10^6) \times (2 \times 10^3) = 8 \times 10^{(6+3)} = 8 \times 10^9$
4	A and C	$(4.0 \times 10^3)(5.0 \times 10^5) = (4 \times 5) \times (10^{3+5}) = 20 \times 10^8 = 2.0 \times 10^9$. Therefore option (A) is correct. $(4.5 \times 10^5) / (9.0 \times 10^9) = (45 \times 10^4)/(9 \times 10^9) = (45/9) \times 10^{4-9} = 5.0 \times 10^{-5}$. This is not equal to 2.0×10^4. Therefore, option (B) is incorrect. $(2.1 \times 10^5) + (2.7 \times 10^5) = (2.1 + 2.7) \times 10^5 = 4.8 \times 10^5$. Therefore option (C) is correct. (3.1×10^5) - $(2.7 \times 10^2) = (3.1 \times 10^3 - 2.7) \times 102 = (3100 - 2.7) \times 10^2 = (3097.3) \times 10^2 = 3.097 \times 10^5$. This is not equal to 0.4×10^3. Therefore option (D) is incorrect.
5	A	Answer choice A is correct. The setting is usually introduced in the introduction or exposition. Note: the setting may change throughout the course of the story. Answer choices B, C, and D are incorrect as the setting is usually introduced in the introduction or exposition of the story.
6	A	Answer choice A is correct. Stories can have more than one setting as the characters move through the story. Answer choice B, C, and D are incorrect.

Week 2

Question No.	Answer	Detailed Explanation
7	C	Answer choice C is correct. The setting of a story can be relayed through the culture of the characters. Answer choices A, B, and D are incorrect.
8	-	There is not enough information to determine the setting of this excerpt as it is a description of a character.

Week 2

Question No.	Answer	Detailed Explanation
1	C	Unit rate means cost per unit (one). "Per" means to divide; so we divide the total cost by the number of units. $1440 ÷ 12 = $120 per unit
2	B	$2.90 ÷ 10 = $0.29 per piece $6.20 ÷ 20 = $0.31 per piece Therefore, Fruity is $0.02 more per piece than Big Bubbles.
3	A	Slope is defined as change in vertical height per unit change in horizontal distance. 9 ft ÷ 54 ft = $\frac{1}{6}$; 12 ft ÷ 84 ft = $\frac{1}{7}$ Since $\frac{1}{6} > \frac{1}{7}$, the first slope is steeper.
4	y=14	To solve this proportion you will have to use cross products. You will multiply the numerator of one to the denominator of the other and the denomiator of the first to the numerator of the second. In this case we would have 7x4=2y. So 28=2y. Next you want to get the variable alone, so you have to use inverse operations to move the 2. In this case we will divide both sides by 2. Thus leaving us with y=14.
5	A	Answer choice A is correct. A round character is one who has many personality traits and is rather complex. Round characters tend to be more involved in the story. Answer choices B, C, and D are incorrect.
6	A	Answer choice A is correct. The protagonist of a story is the main character. This character is who propels the story forward. Answer choices B, C, and D are incorrect.
7	B	Answer choice B is correct. The antagonist of a story is opposing force to the main character or protagonist. The antagonist is not always a character. It may be fate or something in nature. Answer choices A, C, and D are incorrect.

Week 2

Question No.	Answer	Detailed Explanation
8.A	A	Answer choice A is the correct answer. The narrator is the major character in the story because she is the most important character and propels the story forward. The narrator is also the protagonist. Answer choices B, C and D are incorrect.
8.B	D	Answer choice D is correct. The antagonist in this story is the lack of money for the graduation ceremony. The protagonist works to earn money for the ceremony only to find it more difficult than anticipated. In this case, the antagonist is not a who, but a what. Remember the antagonist can be a force which is in direct conflict with the protagonist.

Day 3

Question No.	Answer	Detailed Explanation
1	D	Only the last statement, "Slope is determined by dividing the vertical distance between two points by the corresponding horizontal distance," is true.
2	D	The slope of the line passing through these two points is $\frac{4-2}{-1-1}$ $= \frac{2}{-2} = -1$. The only equation with a slope of -1 is $y = -x + 3$.
3	D	The slope of $y = 4x + 3$ is 4. The slope of $y = 4x - 2$ is 4.
4	The slope is $=\frac{13}{12}$	To find the slope between 2 ordered pairs you use the formula. $\frac{y_2 - y_1}{x_2 - x_1}$ This would look like $\frac{8-(-5)}{0-(-12)} = \frac{13}{12}$ So the slope between the two points is $\frac{13}{12}$
5	B	The story states that Charlie's parents assigned him chores around the house. Because that is not letting Charlie do whatever he wants, answer choice A is incorrect. Also, because he has been earning good grades, it is logical that his parents expect him to continue to earn good grades. Answer choices C and D are incorrect.
6.A	B	Answer choice B is correct. Charlie shoves all his laundry into the machine at once which was not part of the laundry instructions his mom gave him. Answer choice A, C, and D could be true, but the reader must consider only the excerpt provided.
6.B	A	Answer choice A is correct. Because of Charlie's reaction to his shrunken, miscolored clothes, it is evident he doesn't overreact when faced with obstacles but works to find solutions. Answer choices B, C, and D are incorrect.

Week 2

Question No.	Answer	Detailed Explanation
7	B	Answer choice B is correct. Dickens (the author) includes this dialogue so the reader completely understands Scrooge's change in attitude toward Chrismas during the story. Answer choices A, C, and D are incorrect.
8	A	Answer choice A is correct. This dialogue is important because it allows the reader to see the change Scrooge underwent throughout the course of the story. Readers can learn much about characters through their dialogue. Answer choices B, C, and D are incorrect.

Week 2

Question No.	Answer	Detailed Explanation
1	A	Consecutive odd integers lie 2 units apart on the number line; so let the numbers be represented by n and n+2. Their sum is 44; so n + n + 2 = 44. 2n +2 = 44 2n = 44 - 2 2n = 42 n = 21; so n + 2 = 23
2	A	Cumulative GPA $=\dfrac{2.1 +2.9 +3.1 + n}{4}$ $3.0 =\dfrac{8.1 + n}{4}$ $12.0 = 8.1 + n$ $3.9 = n$
3	C	Let m = miles/day for remaining 3 days m = (original miles - miles already traveled) / 3 $m = \dfrac{1924 - 490}{3} = \dfrac{1434}{3} = 478$ miles per day
4	A, C & D	To solve these equations you will use your inverse operations. Depending on if it is a one step or two step you might use one or two operations. The first one is a one step equation. Since it is a multiplcation problem, you will use division to undo it. In this case we are going to divide both sides by -5. When we do this, we get m = -5. The second one is also a one step equation. We divide both sides by -10. When we do this, we get c = 8. The third one is a one step equaion. Since it is a addition problem, to undo the addition, we will subtract. When we subtract a -7 from both sides, we end up with g = -5. The last one is a two step equation. In this case we have to subtract 20 from both sides first. We end up with 12m = -60. Now we have to undo the multiplication. To do this we will divide both sides by 12. When we do this, we will end up with m = -5.

Week 2

Question No.	Answer	Detailed Explanation
5	C	Answer choice C is correct. Tone tells the reader the way the author feels about the topic. Tone can be sad, excited, angry, and humorous - really, just about any emotion. Tone is expressed through word choice or phrasing and sometimes uses figurative language. One way to determine the tone of a piece of writing is to ask yourself how the author feels about the topic he or she has written. Answer choices A, B and D are incorrect.
6	A	Answer choice A is correct. The statement about tone is neutral or indifferent, meaning the writer did not include any language that relays his or her attitude toward the homework assignment. It is just a statement of fact. Answer choice B, C and D are incorrect because the correct tone is neutral.
7	C	Answer choice C is correct. The author's tone is sarcastic which inspires a slightly humorous atmosphere although he is clearly unhappy about the assignment. Answer choices A, B, and D are incorrect.
8.A	A	Answer choice A is correct. The ungrateful son does not want to share the chicken with his father so he hastily, or quickly, hides it. Decisions made in haste can often end up being poor decisions. Hasty decisions are quick and done without much thought. Answer choices B, C, and D are incorrect.
8.B	C	Answer choice C is correct. The frog looked venomously or angrily if someone tried to remove it. Answer choices A, B, and D are incorrect.

Day 5

Question No.	Answer	Detailed Explanation
1	C	$\frac{7}{14} = n + (\frac{7}{14})$ (n) $\frac{1}{2} = n + (\frac{1}{2})$ n; Multiply by 2 to eliminate denominators. $1 = 2n + n$ $1 = 3n$ $\frac{1}{3} = n$
2	B	$2(2x - 7) = 14$ $4x - 14 = 14$ $4x = 14 + 14$ $4x = 28$ $x = 7$
3	D	$6x - (2x + 5) = 11$ $6x - 2x - 5 = 11$ $4x - 5 = 11$ $4x = 11 + 5$ $4x = 16$ $x = 4$
4	A and C	A and C are correct options. You will solve these equations the same way you did when working with integers. To start with the first one you need to get the variable alone so you add $\frac{2}{5}$ to both sides. When you do this you are left with $w = \frac{10}{5}$, which simplifies to w=2. The third one is still dealing with rational numbers, but this time in the form of decimals. First step is to get the variables on one side and the numbers on the other. So, first you will add 1.2 to both sides. You get $0.4x = 0.15x + 2$. Next move the variables to one side. You will subtract 0.15x from both sides. This will leave you with $0.25x = 2$. Last step is to divde both sides by 0.25 (or multiply by 4), and you are left with $x = 8$.

Week 2

Question No.	Answer	Detailed Explanation
5	A	The correct answer is A. When you are comparing, you are looking for similarities. When looking at two pieces of text, if you are asked to compare them, you are being asked to look for what is similar within the two pieces of text. Answer choices B, C, and D are incorrect.
6	C	Answer choice C is correct. A paper or article that is comparing two things will likely use signal words such as likewise, as well, the same as, both, similarly, or too. These are not the only signal words, but they are quite common. Answer choices A, B, and D are incorrect.
7	A	Answer choice A is correct. A Venn diagram provides space for both comparing (the center where the circle meet) and contrasting (the outer circles). Answer choices B, C, and D are incorrect.
8.A	A	Answer choice A is correct. When reading text, it is important to read everything on the page, including the dates. Answer choices B, C, and D are incorrect.
8.B	C	Answer C is correct. When considering both poems, only "The Mountain and the Squirrel" include dialogue. Additionally, the point of view in each point is different. "The Mountain and the Squirrel" is written in third person point of view. "The Song and the Arrow is written in first person point of view.

Question No.	Answer	Detailed Explanation
1	D	$x - 5 = 2x + 1$ $-5 - 1 = 2x - x$ $-6 = x$ Then $y = x - 5$ $y = -6 - 5$ $y = -11$
2	C	These lines have the same slope, but different y-intercepts, so they do not intersect. There is no solution. The lines are parallel.
3	D	$y = 2(2 - 3x) = -6x + 4$ $y = -3(2x + 3) = -6x - 9$ There is no solution because for any value for x, we have 2 different values for y. This is inconsistent.
4	B	Let x = the number of \$1 bills that he has. Let y = the number of \$5 bills that he has. $x + 5y = 49$ (Eq. 1) $x = y + 1$ $x - y = 1$. Multiplying this equation by 5, we get $5x - 5y = 5$ (Eq. 2) Adding Eq. 1 and Eq. 2, $6x = 54$ $x = 9$ (\$1 bills) Substituting $x = 9$ in $x - y = 1$, we get, $y = 8$ (\$5 bills)

Week 3

Day 1

Question No.	Answer	Detailed Explanation
5	D	Answer choice D is correct. All of the choices are puns.
6	D	Answer choice D is correct. Irony, puns, setting and situation can all add humor to a story.
7	C	Answer choice C is correct. Irony is a surprising funny, or interesting contradiction. It is a situation that occurs which is the opposite of what is expected to occur. Answer choices A, B, and D are incorrect.
8	Noise	This scene describes the type of noises not to be afraid of.

Week 3

Question No.	Answer	Detailed Explanation
1	A	$13x + 3y = 15$ $4x + y = 5$ Multiply bottom equation by - 3 and $-12x - 3y = -15$; Add first and last equations. $x = 0$ $x = 0$ Substitute into $y = 5 - 4x$ and $y = 5 - 0$ $y = 5$
2	A	$y = 2x + 5$ $y = 3x - 7$ $2x + 5 = 3x - 7$ $5 = 3x - 7 - 2x$ $5 + 7 = 3x - 2x$ $12 = x$ $y = 2(12) + 5 = 24 + 5 = 29$
3	A	Adding the two equations, we get $4x = 4$; $x = 1$ Then substituting into $2x + 3y = 14$, we get $2 + 3y = 14$ $3y = 14 - 2$ $3y = 12$ $y = 4$
4	A and C	These systems of equations [options (A) and (C)] will intersect at exactly one point. If you solve the first one, it will intersect at (-4, -2). The other one will intersect will intersect at (3, -2). System of equations in the option (B) represents pair of parallel lines as they have same slope but different y - intercept. System of equations in option (D) represent the same line as they have same slope and same y - intercept. So this system have infinite solutions. (Note that the equation $4y = 2x - 4$ is essentially same as $-x + 2y = -2$, when you take out the common factor 2 and rearrange the terms).

Week 3

Question No.	Answer	Detailed Explanation
5	A	Answer choice A is correct because a video allows people to see a visualization.
6	C	Answer choice C is correct. Media can aide an audience seeing and hearing.
7	A	Answer choice A is correct. Since the question is asking for a visual interpretation, a movie will show viewers the interpretation of the director.
8.A	A	Answer choice A is correct because the image is only of the lake. The poem speaks of the lake, but it speaks more of the boy's memories associated with the lake.
8.B	B	Answer choice B is correct because the poem talks about both sounds and sights.

Day 3

Question No.	Answer	Detailed Explanation
1	C	Jorge: $y = 50 + 1x$ Jillian: $y = 72 + .12x$ $50 + 1x = 72 + .12x$ $.88x = 22$ $x = 25$
2	B	Now: Tom = x; Mr. Stevens = y and $y = x + 63$ In 3 Yrs: Tom = x + 3; Mr. Stevens = y + 3 and $y + 3 = 4(x + 3)$ Simplify $y + 3 = 4(x + 3)$ $y = 4x + 12 - 3$ $y = 4x + 9$ and then our system of equations is $y = x + 63$ and $y = 4x + 9$ Multiply top equation by - 4 and $- 4y = -4x - 252$; Add $\underline{y = 4x + 9}$ $-3y = - 243$ $y = 81$ Substitute into $y = x + 63$ $81 = x + 63$ and $18 = x$ which is Tom's age The correct answer is 18 years.
3	C	There are a total of 50 textbooks and workbooks in the box; so t + w = 50. Each textbook weighs 2 lb and each workbook weighs 0.5 lb and the total weight is 55 lb; so 2t + 0.5w = 55.

Question No.	Answer	Detailed Explanation
4	B and C	Options B & C are correct answers.
		You know it has to be the second set of systems because the top one is talking about money so it has to include the cost of tickets and the total cost of tickets. The second equation involves all the people that are at the park that day. The people either are adults or children. Thus making the second one. When solved by elimination you find out that 620 adults are there and 880.
5	D	Answer choice D is correct. A motif is an element or idea in a story that recurs in traditional stories. Motifs can be characters, places, objects, actions or even style.
6	D	Answer choice D is correct. While these are not all the motifs found in traditional stories, they encompass the majority of those stories. Consider the books and stories you read now. Can you find motifs in those that are similar to the motifs in traditional stories? If so, chances are what you are reading is a modern day retelling of a traditional story.
7	C	Answer choice C is correct. The lesson, or moral, of the story is to work hard and prepare for the future. The grasshopper chose to play while the ants worked hard to gather food for the upcoming winter. Once the cold arrived, the grasshopper had nothing to eat, while the ants had plenty because they prepared.
8	A	Answer choice A is correct. Modern day Cinderellas are people who overcome odds and become successful.

Day 4

Question No.	Answer	Detailed Explanation
1	D	In order to be classified as a function each x must map to one and only one value of y. In the case of the set of ordered pairs {(2, 3), (2, 7), (8, 6)}, the x value of 2 has two different values for y, 3 and 7. Therefore, this set does not classify as a function.
2	B	In the case of | x	y
---	---
1	7
3	8
4	7	 for each x there is one and only one value for y. Therefore, this table represents a function.
3	A	If y is a function of x, a particular x value CANNOT be associated with two or more values of y.
4	A and C	If a set of ordered pairs is a function then it will have each x-value going to only one y-value. If an x-value is paired with more than one y-value, then it is not a function.
5	B	Answer choice B is correct. It is the definition of inference.
6	C	Answer choice C is correct. The proper way to cite evidence from a text is to put it in quotes.
7	D	Answer D is the correct choice. All three methods are acceptable ways of citing evidence.

Question No.	Answer	Detailed Explanation
8.A	D	Answer choice D is correct because it describes the first experiment the Montgolfier brothers did with a silk bag and fire. Answer choice A is incorrect because it provides information about the brothers' interests. Answer choice B is incorrect because it explains how Joseph Montgolfier conceived the idea of using hot air to propel an object. The idea came from an observation, not an experiment. Answer choice C is incorrect because it refers to other experiments, not the first one.
8.B	B	Answer choice B is correct because it shows how Joseph observed something as small as pieces of paper floating up the chimney. Answer choice A is incorrect because it describes the materials used to build the balloon. Answer choice C is incorrect because there is no text evidence to support this answer. The passage does not indicate that the Montgolfier's village was the best place to launch their balloon. Answer choice D is incorrect because it simply gives the reader information about Josepeh Montgolfier's interest in flying.

Week 3

Question No.	Answer	Detailed Explanation
1	A	Only p = 2(n – 5) meets the requirements to subtract 5 from n and then double the result to get p.
2	B	The slope is 2. The only function with a slope of 2 is y = 2x + 5.
3	B	According to the table, when x increases by 1, y increases by 2. Therefore the slope of the line (m) is 2. The only function offered with a slope of 2 is y = 2x - 4.
4	Rate of change of function < [Rate of change of function g]	For the function y = 100x, you know the rate of change is 100, so you need to find out the rate of change of the other one. To do this you will have to find the slope, $\frac{180-0}{3-0}$ which is equal to 60. So in this case we are comparing 60 and 100. Since 60 is smaller than 100 the inequality symbol should be < (less than) for this situation.
5	D	Answer choice D is correct. The central idea is the main idea in a piece of informational text. Answer choice A is incorrect because the central idea may not be easily located in the topic sentence. Answer choice B is incorrect because a central idea is located in informational text rather than literature which is generally fiction. Answer choice C is incorrect because an informational piece may not be about a person.
6	D	Answer choice D is correct. The central idea is supported by details in the text; It can sometimes be found in the title of the text, and covers the whole text.
7	D	Answer choice D is correct. When determining the main idea, it is important not to confuse the main idea with the topic (what the passage is about) and the supporting details. The supporting details work to support the main idea.
8	C	Answer choice C is correct. This passage is mainly about learning how to ride a two wheel bike. It does not give instrutctions, but rather describes the process.

Day 1

Question No.	Answer	Detailed Explanation
1	D	The slope of the line through the given points is $\frac{1}{2}$. So slope (m) = $\frac{11 - 7}{k - 6}$ = $\frac{1}{2}$ k-6 = 2(11-7) k-6 = 8 k = 14
2	C	In linear equations, none of the variables is of the second power or higher and they can be put into the form of y = mx + b.
3	B	In the function f(x) = x - 3, the coordinates of (3,0) satisfy the equation and it is written in the form of a linear equation.
4	Non Linear	This function will be non-linear because if we rearrange to solve for y, you will still have x to the second power. Thus making it non-linear.
5	B	Answer B is correct. To find distinctions is to find differences.
6	A	Answer choice A is correct. A connection is a similarity between the reader and something he understands.
7	D	Answer choice D is correct. They both focus on all of the above.
8.A	D	Answer D is correct. They are all ways that marathons are different than other competitions.
8.B	A	Answer A is correct. The article mentions in the beginning that it's not competitive; therefore, answers B and C are incorrect.

Week 4

Question No.	Answer	Detailed Explanation
1	D	There is not enough information to say any of the choices MUST be true although it may represent a portion of the graph of a constant function.
2	A	$y = mx + 2$ $0 = 4m + 2$ $-2 = 4m$ $-\dfrac{2}{4} = m$ $-\dfrac{1}{2} = m$ Therefore, m is negative is true.
3	A	$y = 2x + b$ $0 = 2(-5) + b$ $0 = -10 + b$ $10 = b$ Therefore, b is positive is true.

| 4 | - |

	$y=-4x-3$	$y=7x-5$	$y=-x+2$
(1, 2) slope=7	○	◉	○
(-2, 5) slope=-4	◉	○	○
(3, -1) slope=-1	○	○	◉

Using the slope and an ordered pair you will have to solve for the y-intercept. To do this you will substitute the ordered pair in for x and y into an equation in the format y=mx+b. Once you have this substituted in you will solve for b. This will then give you the equation.

Alternate Explanation : Slope of the line y = mx + b is m (coefficient of x). In this particular problem, since the slopes of the three lines are different, you can easily guess the equations without doing any calculation.

| 5 | B | Answer choice B is correct. A connotation is the meaning of the word with regard to its use in context. |

Day 2

Question No.	Answer	Detailed Explanation
6	A	Detonation means the actual meaning of a word. In other words, it is the dictionary definition of the word. Hence, answer choice A is correct.
7	C	Answer choice C is correct. To trek means to walk a long distance.
8.A	A	Answer choice A is correct. Readers can assume they are ranks in the military because the narrator is on a military ship traveling to a battle.
8.B	A	Answer choice A is the correct answer. The various references to the theater imply that he is comparing a theater to war. Hence, it is an implied metaphor.

Question No.	Answer	Detailed Explanation
1	B	The cost per copy is a function of the number of copies purchased means that the cost per copy changes as the number of copies changes.
2	B	In a positive function, as one variable increases so does the other.
3	C	Her first score was i. She doubled the previous score three times or 2^3i.

| 4 | - |

	INCREASING	DECREASING	CONSTANT
A to B	●	○	○
B to C	●	○	○
G to H	○	○	●
I to J	○	○	●
J to K	○	●	○
K to L	○	●	○
C to D	○	○	●
E to F	○	○	●
D to E	○	●	○
F to G	●	○	○
H to I	○	●	○

If a graph is increasing it will be going from a lower starting point to a higher ending point. If the segment of the graph is decreasing, then it's starting point will be higher than the ending point. If the segement of the graph is constant, then the starting point and ending point will be at the same level.

| 5 | D | Answer choice D is correct. When trying to determine the structure of a piece of text, it is important to look at the genre of writing, the author's purpose and the types of transition words use. |

Question No.	Answer	Detailed Explanation
6	B	Answer choice B is correct. Unlike nonfiction, a fictional story will have a plot.
7	B	Answer choice B is correct. Words such as "unlike", "as well as", "on the other hand", and "in contrast", are all indicative of a comparison.
8.A	B	Answer choice B is correct. Both passages are about learning more about the past. Answer choices A, C, and D are incorrect.
8.B	A	Answer choice A is correct. Both passages discuss human life in the past. "Archaeology" is about the study of past life and "History of Mankind" is about the events in history and how we learn about them today. Answer choices B, C, and D are incorrect.

Week 4

Question No.	Answer	Detailed Explanation
1	D	If you rotate (4,3) 90° clockwise, it will move from quadrant I to quadrant IV. x becomes 3 and y becomes -4.
2	D	There is not enough information provided. All three of the transformations listed would keep the length of the segment the same.
3	A	x becomes -x and y becomes -y as the point rotates from quadrant I to quadrant III.
4	(x,y)---> (x-3, y+4)	In this case since you are translating left, you will need to put a subtraction sign in the first box. In the second box, since you are moving up, you will need to put an addition sign in there.
5	B	Answer choice B is correct. Point of view is the perspective from which the story or text is written.
6	A	Answer choice A is correct. First person point of view is written from the narrator's point of view and will include personal pronouns.
7	A	Answer choice A is correct. When the narrator is in the story, in other words, he or she is telling the story, the story is being told from the first person point of view.
8	B	Answer choice B is correct. Advertisements are created to convince readers or viewers to purchase the item or items being advertised.

Question No.	Answer	Detailed Explanation
1	D	Corresponding angles are congruent under rigid transformations. Since triangle BDE is a reflection image of triangle ABC, and angle C corresponds to angle E, the two angles are equal in measure.
2	D	Corresponding angles are congruent under rigid transformations. Since triangle DEF is a rotated image of triangle ABC, and angle C corresponds to angle F, the two angles are equal in measure.
3	B	Since figure VWXYZ is a rotated image of figure ABCDE, this transformation will prove angle ABC is congruent to angle XYZ.

| 4 | - | |

	30°	60°	90°
Translation	●	○	○
Reflection	●	○	○
Rotation	●	○	○
Dilation	●	○	○

Angle measures will stay the same no matter what transformation it undergoes.

5	D	Answer choice D is correct. When reading text online, it is important to evaluate the source of the information, author's purpose, and date of the source.
6	A	Answer choice A is correct. The fastest place to publish and get public responses is on a webpage on the internet.
7	D	Answer choice D is correct. The best place, and likeliest to reach the most readers, is via a teen magazine AND a website targeting teen audiences.
8	A	Answer choice A is correct. If you need a specific recipe in a hurry, the fastest place to get the information is by doing a web search on the Internet. You can use specific terms which should then navigate you to the appropriate sites.

Week 5

Question No.	Answer	Detailed Explanation
1	B	This is a translation, since the two segments are still oriented in the same way. They were just shifted downward in the coordinate grid.
2	D	This transformation is not a translation, since the line segments are now directed differently. It could be a reflection or a rotation, since both would change the way the segments are facing.
3	D	This transformation is not a translation, since the line segments are now directed differently. It could be a reflection or a rotation, since both would change the way the segments are facing.

4 **-**

	Lengths of sides	Angle Measures	Parallel Sides on Figure
Translation	☑	☑	☑
Reflection	☑	☑	☑
Rotation	☑	☑	☑
Dilation	☐	☑	☑

All of the transformations will preserve the angle measures. Parallel sides of the figure is also preserved i.e. parallel lines remain parallel under all the transformations. Lengths of the sides will change when a figure undergoes a dilation. In other three transformations, lengths of sides is also preserved.

These are all properties of these different transformations. All of them will preserve the angle measures and whether or not the parallel sides will stay parallel. The only thing that they all don't have is that the side lengths will change when a figure undergoes a dilation.

| 5 | A | Answer choice A is correct. An author's claim is something an author is trying to convince you of that hasn't been proven. Once proven, it becomes a fact. |

Day 1

Question No.	Answer	Detailed Explanation
6	B	Answer choice B is correct. When evaluating an author's claim, you must be a careful reader of the support he or she provides for the claim.
7	D	Answer choice D is correct. If you are in doubt of an author's claim, do some research on your own. Look up information on the internet using sites that are dependable or use other research tools such as books and encyclopedias.
8	Unsupported opinion	While people who live in Texas may claim this to be true, this is an unsupported opinion.

Day 2

Question No.	Answer	Detailed Explanation
1	B	Of the choices given, the wings of a butterfly are nearly always congruent; i.e. the same shape and the same size.
2	B	Reflection preserves congruence.
3	D	We can't tell if it was a reflection across the y-axis or a translation.
4	IJKL	If you apply the transformation to the original figure you will see that quadrilater ABCD will land directly on top of quadrilateral IJKL. This will also show that the quadrilaterals will be congruent.
5	D	Answer choice D is correct. When faced with conflicting information, it is a good idea to do further research. Remember, facts can sometimes change. For example, advances in medicine can change what we believe are facts about health. Additionally, checking the credibility of the authors is a good idea.
6	A	Answer choice A is correct. Geology is a science and this can be verified or proven.
7	B	Answer choice B is correct. Whether or not the president's sweater is too small is an opinion. Some people may prefer a snugger fit than others. The conflicting information is based on opinion.
8	Fact	The color of Bailey's shoes can be proven.

Week 5

Question No.	Answer	Detailed Explanation
1	C	A translation slides a figure or point without any alterations in size or shape.
2	A	Triangle A has been rotated to produce triangle B.
3	B	Triangle A has been reflected to produce triangle B.
4	-	(see table and explanation below)

	A(4, -2)	A(-2, 1)	A(-4, -2)
Translation (x+2, y-1)	○	●	○
Rotation 180°	●	○	○
Reflection over x-axis	○	○	●

By applying each one of the transformations to the pre-image, you can come up with the ordered pair for point A. If you translate the original point (-4,2) 2 to the right and one down you end up with (-2,1). If it is a 180 degree rotation you take the opposite of your x-coordinate and the opposite of the y-coordinate. Thus ending up with (4,-2). Finally, if it is a reflection over the x-axis your x-coordinate stays the same and you take the opposite of your y-coordinate. Thus ending up with (-4,-2).

Question No.	Answer	Detailed Explanation
5	B	Answer choice B is correct. An adjective describes or modifies a noun in a sentence.
6	D	Answer choice D is correct. An adverb can modify an adjective, verb, or another adverb in a sentence.
7	D	Answer choice D is correct. The word "good" is an adjective that is used to describe a person, place, thing, or idea. The word "well" is an adverb that is used to explain how something is done.
8	new	The word "new" describes the slide.

Question No.	Answer	Detailed Explanation
1	D	A dilation could transform Triangle A to Triangle B because it shrinks or enlarges a figure.
2	C	The large object has been translated and dilated to produce the smaller object.
3	A	Since the shape of the object has changed, it was not produced by any of the four transformations.

Question 4 —

	Used	Similar only	Congruent
Translation	☑	☐	☑
Rotation	☐	☐	☑
Reflection	☐	☐	☑
Dilation	☑	☑	☐

You can translate to line them up. Whenever you translate you keep the same shape and size, so the figures are congruent. Next, you know you have to dilate because the sizes are different. Whenever you dilate it keeps the same shape, but changes the size. Thus keeping the figures similar.

Question No.	Answer	Detailed Explanation
5	B	Answer choice B is correct. When subjects are connected by "or", the subject closest to the verb determines whether the verb is plural or singular.
6	A	Answer choice A is correct. When there is more than one subject, where one is singular and the other is plural (cat and dogs), the verb (have) will match the subject that is closest to it. So, if the sentence was written as, "Neither the dogs nor the cat...", the verb would be "has" because the subject "cat" is singular. The sentence would read like this, "Neither the dogs nor the cat has been fed".
7	A	Answer choice A is correct. When subjects are connected by "or", the subject closest to the verb determines whether the verb is plural or singular.
8	are	The nouns in the subject are plural; therefore the verb must also be plural.

Week 5

Question No.	Answer	Detailed Explanation
1	D	The statement in the problem is the definition of vertical angles.
2	C	$a + b + c = 180$ $100 + c = 180$ $c = 80°$
3	C	If two parallel lines are cut by a transversal, the corresponding angles are congruent.

Question 4:

	2520	1080	1440	4140	540
Decagon	○	○	●	○	○
16-gon	●	○	○	○	○
Pentagon	○	○	○	○	●
25-gon	○	○	○	●	○
Octagon	○	●	○	○	○

To find the sum of the interior angles of a polygon, you use the formula the number of sides minus 2 times 180. If n is the number of sides (or interior angles), then sum of the interior angles of the polygon = $(n - 2) \times 180°$.

(1) For Decagon, n = 10, sum of the interior angles = $(10 - 2) \times 180° = 1440°$

(2) For 16-gon, n = 16, sum of the interior angles = $(16 - 2) \times 180° = 2520°$

(3) For Pentagon, n = 5. sum of the interior angles = $(5 - 2) \times 180° = 540°$

(4) For 25-gon, n = 25, sum of the interior angles = $(25 - 2) \times 180° = 4140°$

(5) For Octagon, n = 8, sum of the interior angles = $(8 - 2) \times 180° = 1080°$

Question No.	Answer	Detailed Explanation
5	B	Answer choice B is correct. When a pronoun and a noun are used together, choose the pronoun that would fit best if the noun were not there. Answer choice A is incorrect because "we" would not fit without the noun students.
6	A	Answer choice A is correct. "I" is the correct answer. One way to test whether you have the correct answer is to write the sentence out using only the pronoun you are testing and the object. For example, to test the word, "I", you would write, "I enjoyed spending the day at the fair". In contrast, if you were to test the word, "me" you would write, "Me enjoyed spending the day at the fair". This is not correct.
7	D	Answer choice D is correct. When a pronoun and a noun are combined (which will happen with the plural first- and second-person pronouns), choose the case of the pronoun that would be appropriate if the noun were not there.
8	her, her	The pronoun "her" is used twice and refers to Julie.

Day 1

Question No.	Answer	Detailed Explanation
1	C	$3^2+4^2=5^2$ $9+16=25$ $25=25$
2	B	$8^2+15^2=c^2$ $64+225=c^2$ $289=c^2$ $17\text{ cm}=c$
3	C	$7^2+11^2=c^2$ $49+121=c^2$ $170=c^2$ $13.0\approx c$
4	B	In order to solve this equation, you need to have 15 as the hypotenuse. This means that it is one the opposite side of the equal sign. The equation you should select is $4^2 + x^2 = 15^2$.
5	A	Answer choice A is correct. An infinitive phrase always begins with the word "to" followed by a verb. In this case, the infinitive phrase in the sentence is "To make my birthday special."
6	independent	It is an independent clause because it can stand alone.
7	B	Answer choice B is correct. A subordinate, also called a dependent, clause depends on more words in the sentence. It cannot stand alone and always begins with a subordinate conjunction or a relative pronoun.
8	subordinate	The clause is "an accomplished fisherman." It cannot stand alone; therefore, it is subordinate (or dependent).

Week 6

Question No.	Answer	Detailed Explanation
1	C	$8^2+h^2=17^2$ $h^2=289-64$ $h^2=225$ $h=15$ feet
2	A	Applying the Pythagorean Theorem to this (w, 18, 20) right triangle, $w^2 + 18^2 = 20^2$ is the correct equation.
3	D	$5^2+3^2=$(diagonal of bottom of chest)^2 $\sqrt{34}=$diagonal of bottom of chest $34+9=d^2$ $43=d^2$ $\sqrt{43}$ ft $=d$

4	-		$9^2+x^2=15^2$	$40^2+38^2=x^2$	$9^2+15^2=x^2$	$x^2+38^2=40^2$
		One house is 15 miles due north of the park. Another house is 9 miles due east of the park. How far apart are the houses from each other?	○	○	●	○
		The foot of a ladder is put 9 feet from the wall. If the ladder is 15 feet long how high up the building will the ladder reach?	●	○	○	○
		If you drive your car 40 miles south and then 38 miles east, how far would the shortest route be from your starting point?	○	●	○	○
		The diagonal of a TV is 40 inches. The TV is 38 inches long. How tall is the TV?	○	○	○	●

Question No.	Answer	Detailed Explanation
4 contd...	-	The first story gives you the 2 legs of the triangles. So you will need to use the equation that will solve for the hypotenuse. The second one, the ladder is your hypotenuse, so you will be solving for one of the legs. The third one, they give you the legs, so you are solving for the hypotenuse. The last one, the diagonal is the hypotenuse, so you are solving for a leg.
5	B	Answer choice B is correct. A verbal is a verb that acts as another part of speech, such as an adjective or verb. If the question asked for a definition of "verbal" (instead of "a verbal"), then A would be the correct answer.
6	B	Answer choice B is correct. A participle is a verbal that functions as an adjective and will end with either an -ing, -en, or -ed.
7	B	Answer choice B is correct. Gerunds take the place of nouns in a sentence, and they are made by adding -ing to the original verb.
8	A	Answer choice A is correct. The word "jogging" functions as a noun in this sentence.

Day 3

Question No.	Answer	Detailed Explanation
1	A	$4^2+7^2=d^2$ $65=d^2$; d is approx. 8 m
2	C	Draw the graph. Draw the right triangle with the distance between the points as the hypotenuse. The legs will be 6 units & 8 units. Find the hypotenuse. $8^2+6^2=h^2$ $64+36=h^2$ $100=h^2$; $10=h$
3	B	$4^2+14^2=d^2$ $16+196=d^2$ $212=d^2$ $d=14.6$ (approximately)

4	-		10.8	12.2	13	14.8
		(6, 5) and (-4, 9)	●	○	○	○
		(-8, 0) and (5, -7)	○	○	○	●
		(-4, -9) and (6, -2)	○	●	○	○
		(5, 4) and (12, 15)	○	○	●	○

To find the distance between the two ordered pairs I plotted them on a coordinate grid. After I did that I connected them to form a right triangle. Once I had my right triangles, I could use Pythagorean Theorem to solve for the missing side.

Question No.	Answer	Detailed Explanation
5	A	Answer choice A is correct. The subject comes before the action in active voice.
6	D	Answer choice D is correct. A sentence written in the passive voice means the subject is acted upon instead of doing the action.
7	C	Answer choice C is correct. A sentence written in active voice means the subject of the sentence is performing the action.
8	Active	The subject is doing the action.

Week 6

Question No.	Answer	Detailed Explanation
1	D	$V = \frac{4}{3}(\pi r^3)$ $V = \frac{4}{3}(\pi) 6^3$ $V = \frac{4}{3}(216)\pi$ $V = 288\pi$
2	C	$V = (\frac{1}{3})Bh$ where B= area of the base $V = (\frac{1}{3})\pi(4^2)(9)$ $V = 48\pi$
3	C	$V = \pi r^2 h$ $V = \pi(25)(3)$ $V = 75\pi$
4	75.36 ft³	Radius of the cone = r = 3 ft. Height of the cone = h = 8 ft. Volume of the cone = $V = (1/3)\pi r^2 h$ $V = (1/3) \times 3.14 \times 3^2 \times 8$ $V = 75.36$ ft³
5	A	Answer choice A is correct. Commas are used to separate three or more items in a list.
6	C	Answer choice C is correct. When an appositive is in the middle of a sentence, it must be set off by commas. An appositive is a noun phrase that renames or clarifies the noun.
7	B	Answer choice B is correct. In complex sentences, a subordinating clause is set off with a comma. "After you have finished taking out the trash" is the subordinating clause in the sentence.
8	-	Yvette's invitation for Brenda's surprise party said to bring the following things to the party: cupcakes, soda, and a gag gift. Both names are possessive; a colon is used because a list follows, and commas separate the list.

Day 5

Question No.	Answer	Detailed Explanation
1	B	By definition, a decreasing trend from left to right on a scatter plot indicates a negative association.
2	A	By definition, an increasing line from left to right on a scatter plot indicates a positive association.
3	no association	There is no association between the apple and mango sales. You can see that they neither consistently go up or go down over the course of the 10 days.
4	C	The points in the third choice are nearly in a straight line.
5	A	Answer choice A is correct. An ellipsis is …
6	D	Answer choice D is correct. An ellipsis is used to: * Indicating omissions in quoted material * Indicating hesitation or trailing off in spoken words * Imparting extra significance to a sentence
7	A	Answer choice A is correct. An ellipsis can be used to create suspense.
8	D	Answer choice D is correct. In all of the above examples, an ellipsis would be used.

Week 7

Question No.	Answer	Detailed Explanation
1	D	This scatter plot does not represent a linear function. None of these is the correct choice.
2	C	The line of best fit would be a horizontal line. Constant linear is the correct choice.
3	D	The data does not represent a straight line. None of these is the correct choice.
4	$y=(-3/7)$ $x+45/7$	The best fit line is already drawn on the graph, but they want the equation to go with it. Using the 2 points they gave us we first need to find the slope. $$\frac{6-8}{1-8} = -\frac{3}{7}$$ Now that we know the slope, we can fill in an ordered pair and solve for the y-intercept. $6=-\frac{3}{7}(1)+b$ When you solve for b you get . Put those numbers together and you get the equation . $y=-\frac{3}{7}x+\frac{45}{7}$
5	B	Answer choice B is correct. Homophones, also known as homonyms, are words that are pronounced the same, but have different meanings. Often they are spelled differently, and it is important to learn to use the correct spelling of the word. An example is: threw, through
6	C	Answer choice C is correct. The word "threw" means to propel or hurl an object. The word "through" means to go in one end and out another.
7	B	Answer choice B is correct. The first "they're" is a contraction for "they are." The second "there" refers to a location and the third "their" shows possession.
8	persuade	The correct spelling is persuade.

Day 2

Question No.	Answer	Detailed Explanation
1	A	Visual inspection of the points and lines shows that the first scatter plot is the best choice because it shows a positive association, just like the original scatter plot does. As x increases, y increases.
2	A	The line in choice one passes through the center of the scatter plot with approximately the same number of stray points on each side.
3	D	The line in choice 4 is clearly a best fit line.
4	-	(see table below)

	Linear	Negative Association	Line of Best Fit	Prediction Equation
A line on a graph showing the general direction that a group of points seem to be heading	○	○	●	○
A graph that is represented by a straight line	●	○	○	○
The equation of a line that can predict outcomes using given data	○	○	○	●
A correlation of points that is linear with a negative slope	○	●	○	○

The line that is on the graph that doesn't necessarily go through every point but represents the general trend of the graph would be the line of best fit. If it is a straight line, then it is a linear graph. The equation of the best fit line that helps you predict outcomes are the prediction equation. Lastly, if the trend of the scatter plot has a negative slope then it has a negative association.

Week 7

Question No.	Answer	Detailed Explanation
5	D	Answer choice D is correct. Verbs have mood, tense, and voice.
6	A	Answer choice A is correct. Active is a voice, not a mood.
7	A	Answer choice A is correct. Subjunctive mood suggests an unreal situation.
8	A	Answer choice A is correct because an indicative tone indicates a fact.

Week 7

Question No.	Answer	Detailed Explanation
1	C	Out of 25 people wearing sneakers, 15 were also wearing jeans. $\dfrac{15}{25} = 60\%$ 60% is the correct choice.
2	D	Out of 20 people wearing jeans, 15 were also wearing sneakers. $\dfrac{15}{20} = 75\%$ 75% is the correct choice.
3	B	Out of 25 people not wearing sneakers, 5 were wearing jeans. $\dfrac{5}{25} = \dfrac{1}{5} = 20\%$ 20% is the correct answer.

4 -		131	.60	145	.66
Total number of 7th graders surveyed		○	○	●	○
Total number of 8th graders surveyed		●	○	○	○
The relative frequency of 7th grade students that chose English to all students that chose English		○	●	○	○
The relative frequency of 8th grader students that chose Math to the total number of 8th graders		○	○	○	●

Question No.	Answer	Detailed Explanation
4 contd...	-	To find the total number of 7th graders you add 78 + 67 = 145. To get the total number of 8th graders surveyed add 86 + 45 = 131. To find the relative frequency of the 7th graders that chose English to the total number that chose English take $\frac{67}{(67+45)} = 0.60$ (when rounded to the nearest hundredth). And lastly, to find the relative frequency of the 8th grade students that chose Math to the total number of 8th graders I took $\frac{86}{(86+45)} = 0.66$ (when rounded to the nearest hundredth).
5	A	Answer choice A is correct. Context clues are the words that surround the unknown word. Context clues help the reader determine the meaning of the word.
6	D	Answer choice D is correct. When faced with an unfamiliar word in a story or passage, it is helpful to go back and reread the surrounding text, both before and after the unfamiliar word. The words and phrases that help the reader determine the meaning of the word are called context clues.
7	A	Answer choice A is correct. Context clues can be found at the end of the sentence, "...because he never missed a shot." This means he never made a mistake or error.
8	B	Answer choice B is correct. Context clues are underlined in the sentences: Bailey had a sense of foreboding as she walked into the classroom. She noticed that all the bulletin boards were covered up and the privacy folders were lying on the desks. Had she forgotten a test?

Day 4

Question No.	Answer	Detailed Explanation
1	B	Pi is the ratio of a circle's circumference to its diameter. It is therefore a real number. Pi cannot be expressed as the ratio of two integers, so it is irrational.
2	B	$\sqrt{7}$ cannot be expressed as the ratio of two integers and is therefore irrational. The irrationals are a subset of the real numbers.
3	D	The number 57 meets the requirements of each of the following sets of numbers: N (natural numbers), W (whole numbers), Z (integers), Q (rational numbers), and R (real numbers).
4	C	$\sqrt{10}$ is the irrational number because it cannot be written as a fraction. The others can.
5	B	Answer choice B is correct. Homonyms are words that are considered multiple-meaning words. They are words that share the same spelling and pronunciation but have a different meaning.
6	B	Answer choice B is correct. Homophones are words that sound the same but are spelled differently and have different meanings.
7	C	Answer choice C is correct. Address is a homonym meaning it is a multiple-meaning word.
8	A, E, F	Graduation refers to completion, culmination and closure. Hence, answer choices A, E and F are correct.

Week 7

Question No.	Answer	Detailed Explanation
1	B	$\sqrt{(0.6561)}=.81$ .8... means that the 8 is repeating; i.e. .888... .8 may be written as .80 So .8 represents the smallest (least) value.
2	A	$4\frac{1}{2} = 4.5$ $2 < \sqrt{5} < 3$ $\sqrt{10} > 3$; so $2\sqrt{10} > 6$ Then, the correct order is: $\sqrt{5}$, $4\frac{1}{2}$, 4.75, $2\sqrt{10}$
3	C	$\sqrt{.4}$ =(approx.) .63 which is the greatest of these numbers.
4	B	$\sqrt{.9}$ = (approx.) .95 So $\sqrt{.9}$, .9, .999, .9... is the correct order.
5	B	Answer B is correct. The prefix "pre" means before; therefore, a prefix goes at the beginning of a word.
6	A	Answer choice A is correct. A suffix is the letter blend that goes at the end of a word.
7	B	Answer choice B is correct. An affix is the prefix or suffix that is attached to a root to create a new word.
8	A	someone who announces

Day 1

Question No.	Answer	Detailed Explanation
1	C	$X^{(2-5)} = X^{-3}$ Now move x-3 to the denominator and change the sign of the exponent from negative to positive. $\frac{1}{X^3}$
2	A	Regardless of the number of 1s that we multiply the result is always 1 because 1 is the identity element for multiplication.
3	C	When multiplying quantities with the same base, you add exponents. $(X^{-3})(X^{-3}) = X^{-6}$ To change the exponent -6 to positive 6, you write the reciprocal of X^{-6}. $\frac{1}{X^6}$
4	a^{16}	You are using your product rule to find out the exponent. When using the product rule if the base is the same, then you add the exponents. In this case, you will add $7+8+1=16$. So it would become a^{16}.
5	E	Answer choice E is correct. Questionnaires, experiments, field studies, and scholarly articles are all acceptable references for research. Using a variety of these resources makes for the most reliable research.
6	B	Answer choice B is correct. It is difficult to determine the reliability of one or two sources. When doing research, it is important to constantly ask yourself who wrote the resources you are using and why were they written? Using several sources for research will prove to be most reliable.
7	D	Answer choice D is correct. Use caution when using Internet resources. Make sure the author is reliable and the information is current.
8	D	Answer choice D is correct. Anne Frank's diary was written by her; therefore it is a primary source.

Question No.	Answer	Detailed Explanation
1	A	$10^2 = 100$ and $11^2 = 121$ Therefore, the square root of 110 is between 10 and 11.
2	A	$6\sqrt{20} \div \sqrt{5} = 6\sqrt{4}\sqrt{5} \div \sqrt{5} = 6\sqrt{4} = 12$
3	A	$4^3 = 64$ and $5^3 = 125$ Therefore, the cube root of 66 is between 4 and 5.
4	A and C	Options (A) and (C) are correct, because if you take the cube root of them, you will get an integer. 27 can be written as $3 \times 3 \times 3 = 3^3$. and and 1000 can be written as $10 \times 10 \times 10 = 10^3$. $\sqrt[3]{27} = 3$ $\sqrt[3]{1000} = 10$ 27, 1000 are called perfect cubes.
5	A	Answer A is correct. The context clue is a synonym, "hard work" helps determine the meaning.
6	B	Answer B is correct. The context clues are antonyms, "preparing takes months".
7	C	Answer choice C is correct. The context clue "maintain" shows it must stay the same.
8	B	Answer choice B is correct. A dictionary is the right choice.

Week 8

Question No.	Answer	Detailed Explanation
1	C	From 1.53×10^7, we move the decimal to the right 7 places giving us 15,300,000.
2	B	Move the decimal 3 places to the left.
3	C	$1 \leq N \leq 9.99...$ and we must move the decimal 5 places to the right resulting in $100,000 \leq N \times 10^5 < 1,000,000$.
4	2.347×10^9	The number in the first box has to be a decimal number that is larger than 1, but less than 10. In this case it will be 2.347. Next, we will take it 10 times itself to an exponent which will move our decimal until it becomes our number in standard form. So in this case we have to take 10 times itself 9 times, so our exponent will be 9. Our final answer will be 2.347×10^9
5	B	Answer choice B is correct. Like a simile, a metaphor compares two unlike things; however, it does not use like or as in the comparison. Instead, it just makes the statement. For example: The treacherous road snaked wildly through the canyons. In this sentence, the curves of a dangerous (treacherous) road are being compared to the curves of a snake as it slithers across the ground. You could make this sentence say something similar by using a simile instead of a metaphor: The treacherous road curved like a snake through the canyons. Answer choices A, C, and D are incorrect.
6	C	Answer choice C is correct. Alliteration is the repetition of same letter sounds at the beginning of words or stressed syllables. Onomatopoeia is a sound word like splash, squirt, and plop. Both figures of speech have to do with the sounds of words. Answer choices A, B, and D are incorrect.
7	C	Answer choice C is correct. Remember a metaphor is like a simile, but doesn't use "like" or "as" in the comparison. In this metaphor, the speaker is comparing his blurry thinking to fog. Answer choice A is a simile. Answer choice B is alliteration. Answer choice D is onomatopoeia.
8	simile	Sarah is being compared to a hungry toddler. When toddlers are hungry, they are cranky and generally cry and carry on.

Question No.	Answer	Detailed Explanation
1	D	$(2 \times 10^{-3}) \times (3 \times 10^5) = (2 \times 3) \times 10^{(-3+5)} = 6 \times 10^2$
2	B	$(2.4 \times 10^3) / (6 \times 10) = 0.4 \times 10^2 = 4 \times 10 = 40$
3	A	$(5 \times 10^5) \times (9 \times 10^{-3}) = (45 \times 10^{5-3}) = 45 \times 10^2 = 4.5 \times 10^3$ Therefore, 4.5×10^4 is not equal to 4.5×10^3, so 4.5×10^4 is the correct answer. Options (B), (C) and (D) are different ways of expressing the same number.
4	C and D	In these particular cases it is easy to see which numbers are larger and which are smaller based only on their exponents. If it is a larger number the exponent will be greater. So to get them in order from largest to smallest, look at the exponent and put them in order from largest exponent to the smallest, making sure that when you get into negative powers (or exponents), larger the absolute value of the power, smaller the actual number.
5	B	Answer choice B is correct. An analogy compares two words, specifically two words which can somehow be compared. For example, a heart and a pump. Answer choices A, C, and D are incorrect.
6	C	Answer choice C is correct. This analogy is comparing a part of a tree (branch) to the whole tree. The second half of the analogy compares part of a hand (fingers) to the whole hand. Answer choices A, B, and D are incorrect.
7	A	Answer choice A is correct. The first set of words in the analogy are antonyms, repel and attract are opposite in meaning. Therefore, the second half of the analogy should also have a word set which are antonyms. "Follow" is an antonym to "lead". Answer choices B, C and D are not antonyms to the word lead, therefore are incorrect.
8	-	Hyperbole

Week 8

Question No.	Answer	Detailed Explanation
1	B	$4 \text{ ft} \div 12 \text{ ft} = \frac{1}{3}$ which is the largest ratio so the steepest slope.
2	A	The unit rate can also be called the average or mean, but not the mode, median, nor the frequency.
3	A	Unit cost is calculated by dividing the total cost by the amount of items. This statement is true. Therefore, "Unit cost is calculated by dividing the amount of items by the total cost." must be a false statement. (This would represent the number of items you get per dollar paid.)
4	y=25	To solve this proportion you will have to use cross products. You will multiply the numerator of one to the denominator of the other and the denomiator of the first to the numerator of the second. In this case we will multiply 20x20=16y. 400=16y. Then we have to use inverse operations to get y by iteself. In this case we will divide both sides by 16. We will end up with y=25.
5	B	Answer choice B is correct. This word is used connotatively to describe that the girl doesn't act her age. Immature is a word in which the connotation can vary depending on the words around it. If it were used to describe a very young child, the connotation would be neutral as young children are immature, or the opposite of mature. In this sentence, immature is used to convey a negative idea. Answer choices A and C are incorrect.
6	C	Answer choice C is correct. While none of the words have a negative connotation, home conveys to the reader a place where a family lives and is loved. Answer choices A, B, and D have neutral connotations.
7	A	Answer choice A is correct. In this case, all three words are adjectives used to describe the spending habits of an individual. Being described as cheap has a negative connotation. If you are frugal or thrifty, that means you are careful with your money.
8	Positive	As used in the sentence, the word "screamed" has a positive connotation. The narrator's mom was happy she won first place and, as a result, her scream was happy.

Day 1

Question No.	Answer	Detailed Explanation
1	D	$y = \frac{9}{5}x - 3$ has a slope of $\frac{9}{5}$ which is the greatest.
2	A	$\frac{1}{8}$ is the smallest slope. $y = \frac{1}{8}x + 7$ is the correct answer.
3	A	If we know the y-intercept and the slope, we can write the equation of a straight line. If we know the y-intercept, we know b in the slope-intercept formula. The y-intercept together with another point or the x-intercept make it possible to determine the slope of the line. Direction would not give enough information
4	The slope is $= \frac{1}{9}$	To find the slope between 2 ordered pairs you use the formula $\frac{y_2 - y_1}{x_2 - x_1}$ This would look like $\frac{-2-(-3)}{12-3} = \frac{1}{9}$ So the slope between the two points is $\frac{1}{9}$
5	B	Answer choice B is correct. Jargon is words that are specific to an area of study.
6	D	Answer choice D is correct. All of the examples are specific to literature.
7	A	Answer choice A is correct. A symbol is specific to literature; therefore, it is domain specific.
8	-	Meter is specific to poetry; therefore, it is domain specific.

Week 9

Question No.	Answer	Detailed Explanation
1	C	$3x + 5 = 29$ $3x = 29 - 5$ $3x = 24$ $x = 8$
2	D	$7 - 2x = 13 - 2x$ $7 - 13 = 0$ $-6 = 0$ Since this is a false statement, there is not solution to this equation.
3	B	$6x + 1 = 4x - 3$ $6x - 4x = -3 - 1$ $2x = -4$ $x = -\dfrac{4}{2}$ $x = -2$
4	-8	To solve this 2-step equation you must first get rid of the 20. Since it is adding 20, to undo it you must subtract 20 from both sides. Making it now $5x = -40$. Now the second step is to undo the multiplication. To undo it, we will divide both sides by 5. Ending up with $x = -8$.
5	B	Answer choice B is correct. The first word of every sentence should ALWAYS be capitalized. Answer choice A, grandmother, would be capitalized when it is used as a proper noun. Proper nouns should always be capitalized.
6	B	Answer choice B is correct. In the first sentence, the word "grandmother" is used as a proper noun.
7	D	Answer choice D is correct. Always capitalize historical events, the first letter of a sentence, and all words in the title or name of an organization.
8	France	Only the proper noun, France, should be capitalized. Remember seasons are not capitalized.

Question No.	Answer	Detailed Explanation
1	B	$4x + 2(x - 3) = 0$ $4x + 2x - 6 = 0$ $6x - 6 = 0$ $6x = 6$ $x = 6 \div 6$ $x = 1$
2	A	$3y - 7(y + 5) = y - 35$ $3y - 7y - 35 = y - 35$ $-4y - 35 = y - 35$ $-35 = y - 35 + 4y$ $-35 + 35 = y + 4y$ $0 = 5y$ $0 = y$
3	A	$2(x-5) = \dfrac{1}{2}(6x + 4)$ $2x - 10 = 3x + 2$ $-12 = x$
4		$\dfrac{8}{16} = n + \dfrac{8}{16}n$ Multiplying both sides by 2, we get, $2 \times \dfrac{8}{16} == 2\left(n + \dfrac{8}{16}n\right)$ $1 = 2n + n$ $3n = 1$ Therefore, $n = \dfrac{1}{3}$

Question No.	Answer	Detailed Explanation
5	A	Answer choice A is correct because the poet understands that sympathy is invaluable. Answer choice D is incorrect beacuase it refers to the rich man who gave the poet gold. Answer choices B and C do not provide text evidence to support the gratefulness of the poet.
6	B	Answer choice B is correct. Text evidence supporting this answer can be found in the first stanza, lines 3 and 4. There is no evidence to support answer choices A, C or D.
7	A	Answer choice A is correct because the squirrel is telling the mountain that it's okay for everyone to have their own talent. Answer choice B is incorrect because the squirrel is describing the mountain, not its talent. Answer choice C is incorrect because the squirrel is simply commenting on its own size. Answer choice D is incorrect because the squirrel is commenting on an attribute of the mountain.
8.A	D	Answer choice D is correct. Patrick was in such a hurry he did not check to see if his bag was in the trunk of his car. His mom realized he had left it and ran out to remind him. There is no evidence to support answer choices A, B, or C.
8.B	A	Answer choice A is correct. The word this in the sentence, "he just knew he would make the team this year" indicates that Patrick has tried out before and not made the team. There is no evidence to support answer choices B, C, or D.

Day 4

Question No.	Answer	Detailed Explanation

1   **B**

$\frac{x}{2} + \frac{y}{2} = 2$

$3x - 2y = 48$

Multiplying the first equation by 6 gives $3x + 2y = 12$

Adding to $3x - 2y = 48$ gives $6x = 60$

$x = 10$

$3(10) - 2y = 48$

$30 - 2y = 48$

$-2y = 48 - 30 = 18$

$y = -9$

2   **B**

$y = 2x - 6$

$y = -2x + 6$

$2x - 6 = -2x + 6$

$2x + 2x = 6 + 6$

$4x = 12$

$x = 3$

$y = 2(3) - 6 = 0$

3   **A**

Adding the two equations, we get $4x = 4$; $x = 1$

Then substituting into $2x + 3y = 14$, we get $2 + 3y = 14$

$3y = 14 - 2$

$3y = 12$; $y = 4$

4   **D**

Let x = Cole's age now and y = Anya's age now.

$y = x + 3$. This can be rewritten as $y - x = 3$

$x + 11 = 2y$

$2y - x = 11$ Eqn. 1

Multiplying the equation, $y - x = 3$ by -1, we get

$\underline{-y + x = -3}$ Eqn. 2

Adding Eqn. 1 and Eqn. 2, we get $y = 8$.

Substituting $y = 8$ in, $y - x = 3$, we get $x = 5$.

$y = 8$ years old ; $x = 5$ years old

Week 9

Question No.	Answer	Detailed Explanation
5	C	Answer choice C is correct. Samantha's heart pounding loudly, her friendly smile and blushing all indicate she thought the boy was cute. Answer choices A, B and D are not supported by the text. Nothing in the text referred to the boy's backpack, and the boy's actions were not discussed, so the reader cannot draw an inference based on his behavior.
6	A	Answer choice B is incorrect because Maya realizes the family is needy based on both their actions and the state of their clothes. Hence, answer choice A is correct.
7	B	Answer choice B is correct because Henry has been saving his money for a year and did research on his destination. Answer choice A is incorrect because Henry has been saving his money, so the trip was planned. Answer choice C is incorrect because Henry did research on his destination. Answer choice D cannot be inferred from the text.
8	-	The door was hard to open because it hadn't been opened in quite some time. Additionally, there were cobwebs in the room and dust on the floor meaning no one had entered the room in a long time.

Day 5

Question No.	Answer	Detailed Explanation
1	D	Solving the second equation for x, we get $x = 13 + 2y$ which is identical to the first equation. Therefore, there are infinitely many points (x, y) that satisfy the system.
2	C	Examining these equations we find an inconsistency. $2x + 5y$ CANNOT be equal to two different quantities. Therefore, there is no solution.
3	A	Adding the two equations, we get $14y = 28$. $y = 2$ Substituting into $4x + 7y = 2$, we get $4x + 14 = 2$ $4x = -12$ $x = -3$
4	B, C & D	Options B, C and D are correct answers. These all have no solution because the equations in each of these systems will make parallel lines. Since the lines are parallel, they will not intersect making no solution.
5	C	Answer choice C is correct. Readers should look for details in the story to help determine the theme of the story. It also helps to think about what the main character learns. Answer choices A, B, and D are incorrect as they are not ways to help a reader determine the theme of a story.
6	B	Answer choice B is correct. The reader determines an implied theme of a story through clues in the story. Answer choices A, C, and D are not definitions of an implied theme.

Week 9

Question No.	Answer	Detailed Explanation
7	B	Answer choice B is correct. The Crow learns that she should not be so trusting of someone who lavishes her with compliments. Considered universally, the theme then becomes don't be trusting of flatterers. Answer choices A, C and D are not themes of this story.
8.A	A	Answer choice A is correct. Had the man offered to share his chicken, it would not have turned into a toad forever requiring attention. Answer choices B, C and D are incorrect because none of them are themes of this story.
8.B	A	Answer choice A is correct. The theme is implicitly stated. That is, the reader must use the actions of the man, hiding the roasted chicken so he doesn't have to share, to determine the theme of the text. Answer choices B, C and D are incorrect because they are not reasonable.

STOP! IN THE NAME OF EDUCATION: PREVENT SUMMER LEARNING LOSS WITH 7 SIMPLE STEPS

Summer Learning loss is defined as "a loss of knowledge and skills . . . most commonly due to . . . . extended breaks [during the summertime] " (from edglossary.org/learning-loss). Many teachers have certainly had the experience of taking the first month of school not only to introduce his or her rules and procedures to the class but also to get the kids back "up to speed" with thinking, remembering what they've learned . . . and in many cases, reviewing previous content. With a traditional school calendar, then, this can mean that up to 10% of the school year is spent playing catch-up.

What's a parent to do? Fortunately, there are some simple steps you can take with your child to help your son or daughter both enjoy the summer and keep those all-important skills honed and fresh:

(1) Read!

Research supports the relationship between independent reading and student achievement, so simply having your child read daily will make a positive difference. Check out the following sources to find books that your child will want to dive into: your public library, local bookstores, online stores (Amazon, Barnes and Noble, half.com, etc.), and yard sales (if the family hosting the sale has children a bit older than your own, you stand a good chance of scoring discarded books that are a perfect match for your son or daughter's reading level).

(2) Write!

Have your child write letters to out-of-town friends and family, or write postcards while on vacation. A summer journal is another way to document summer activities. For the artistic or tech-savvy child, you may choose to create a family scrapbook with captions (consider the online options at Shutterfly, Mixbook, and Smilebox). Not only will you preserve this summer's memories, but your child will also continue to practice his or her writing skills! (See Summer is Here! Ideas to Keep Your Child's Writing Skills Sharp for more writing ideas.)

(3) Do the Math!

Think of ways your child can incorporate math skills into daily activities: have a yard sale, and put

your child in charge of the cash box; help younger ones organize a lemonade stand (to practice salesmanship and making change). Or simply purchase a set of inexpensive flash cards to practice basic facts while waiting in line or on a long car ride. There's even a host of free online games that will keep your child's math skills sharp.

(4) "Homeschool" Your Child

Keeping your child's skills fresh doesn't have to cost a fortune: check out some of the Lumos Learning workbooks and online resources (at lumoslearning.com/store), and your child can work through several exercises each day. Even as little as twenty minutes a day can yield positive results, and it's easy to work in a small block of time here and there. For instance, your child can work in the book during a car ride, right before bedtime, etc. Or, simply make this part of your child's morning routine. For example: wake up, eat breakfast, complete chores, and then work in the workbook for 20 minutes. With time, you can make this a natural habit.

(5) Go Back-to-School Shopping (For a Great Summer School Learning Experience)

Check out offerings from the big names (think Sylvan, Huntington, Mathnasium, and Kumon), and also consider local summer schools. Some school districts and local colleges provide learning programs: research the offerings on-line for more information regarding the available options in your area.

(6) Take a Hike . . . Go Camping!

But "camp" doesn't always involve pitching a tent in the great outdoors. Nowadays, there are camps for every interest: sports camps, art camp, music camp, science camp, writing camp . . . the possibilities are endless! With a quick Internet search, you'll be able to turn up multiple options that will appeal to your son or daughter. And even if these camps aren't "academic", the life skills and interpersonal experiences are certain to help your child succeed in the "real world". For example, working together as a cast to put on a summer theater production involves memorizing lines, cooperation, stage crew coordination, and commitment – all skills that can come in handy when it comes to fostering a good work ethic and the ability to collaborate with others.

(7) Get tutored

Many teachers offer tutoring services throughout the summer months, either for individuals or small groups of students. Even the most school-averse student tends to enjoy the personal attention of a former teacher in a setting outside of the classroom. Plus, a tutor can tailor his or her instruction to pinpoint your child's needs – so you can maximize the tutoring sessions with the skills and concepts your child needs the most help with.

Of course, you don't need to do all seven steps to ensure that your child maintains his or her skills. Just following through with one or two of these options will go a long way toward continued learning, skills maintenance, and easing the transition to school when summer draws to a close.

SUMMER READING: QUESTIONS TO ASK THAT PROMOTE COMPREHENSION

As mentioned in our "Beating Summer Academic Loss" article, students are at risk of losing academic ground during the summer months, especially with respect to their reading level, spelling, and vocabulary. One of the best ways to prevent this "brain drain" for literacy is to have your son or daughter read each day during the summer break.

Better yet, you can promote these all-important skills and participate in your child's summer reading by engaging in active dialogue with your son or daughter. Below are several questions and ideas for discussion that will promote comprehension, recall, and critical thinking skills. In addition, these questions reflect several of the Common Core standards – which underpin the curriculum, instruction and standardized testing for most school districts. Of course, the standards vary by grade level, but some of the common themes that emerge in these standards are: citing evidence, summarizing, and making inferences.

• Citing evidence

Simply put, citing evidence involves going back into the text (book, magazine, newspaper, etc.) and finding "proof" to back up an answer, opinion, or assertion. For instance, you could ask your child, "Did you enjoy this book?" and then follow up that "yes" or "no" response with a "Why?" This requires the reader to provide details and examples from the story to support his or her opinion. For this particular question, then, your child may highlight plot events he or she liked, character attributes, writing style, and even genre (type of book) as evidence. Challenge for older students: Ask your child to go back into the text and find a direct quote to support an opinion or answer.

• Summarizing

For nonfiction pieces, this may involve being able to explain the 5W's – who, what, where, when, why (and how). For literature, ask your child to summarize the story elements, including: the setting, characters, main conflict or problem, events, resolution, and theme/lesson/moral. If your child can do this with specificity and accuracy, there's a very good chance that he or she comprehended the story. Challenge for older students: Ask your child to identify more complex story elements, such as the climax, rising action, and falling action.

• Making inferences

Making an inference is commonly referred to as "reading between the lines." That is, the reader can't find the answer to a question directly in the text but instead must synthesize or analyze information to come to a conclusion. To enhance these higher-level thinking skills, ask your child to describe the main character's personality, describe how a character changed by the end of a novel, or detail how the setting influenced the story's plot. Challenge for older students: Have the reader compare and contrast two or more characters to highlight similarities and differences in personality, actions, etc.

 Of course, if you read the same book that your child reads, you'll be able to come up with even more detailed questions – and also know if your child truly understood the reading based on his or her answers! But even if you don't get a chance to read what your child does, simply asking some of these questions not only helps your child's reading skills but also demonstrates an interest in your child – and his or her reading.

BEATING THE BRAIN DRAIN THROUGH COMPUTING: WEBINAR RECAP WITH PRINTABLE ACTIVITY SHEET

Lumos Learning conducted webinar on "Beating the Brain Drain" series. During this interactive workshop, students were given many practical ideas and tips for keeping their math skills sharp in the summertime.

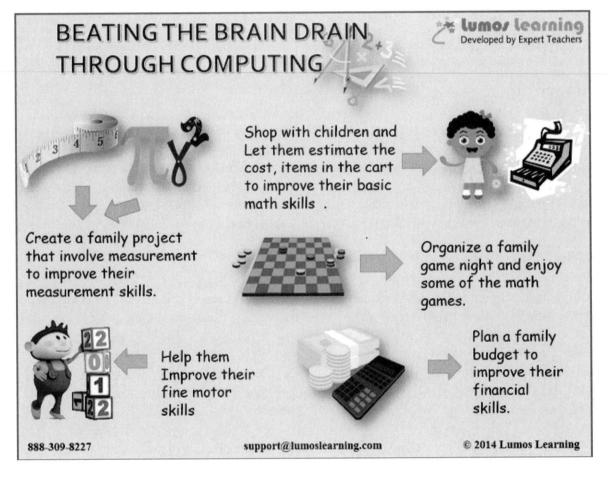

To review the webinar content, use this chart with your child to reinforce his or her math skills. Work together to select ideas that appeal to your son or daughter. And be sure to get involved: many of these suggestions are ideal for two or more people! Please note that there is an additional column so that you can keep track of and check off activities that your child has completed.

Suggested Activity	Skills/Mathematical Concepts	Completed this activity	Notes for parents
Create a family project that involves measurement, basic math calculations, geometry, etc.	Area Perimeter Measurement Basic facts		As a family, decide upon a project that you can do together. Possible project ideas include: creating a family garden, building a bird feeder, or tackling a home improvement project. Ask your child to help list the items you need to purchase at the store, read the directions (if applicable), and help with the installation, building, and measurement. In addition to math skills, your child can improve his or her fine motor skills. Of course, be sure to supervise properly and follow all safety precautions when using tools and equipment.
Go shopping together.	Estimation Addition Subtraction Multiplication Mental math skills		You can shop for back-to-school items – or simply go grocery shopping together. Have your child estimate the total cost of the items in the cart, determine sales tax, and figure out the change (if you're paying in cash).
Budget together.	Financial literacy skills Estimation Addition Subtraction Mental math skills		If your family is planning to take a vacation, ask your child to help with the budget! During the trip, keep all the receipts, and then tally up the cost of the trip. Have your son or daughter break up the trip into categories to track spending, too – food, fun, hotels, gas, etc. As a challenge, your child can calculate what percentage of the budget has been spent on each category.

Track family or individual spending.	Financial literacy skills Addition Subtraction Estimation		Use a blank checkbook register to monitor spending (real or imaginary). You child will need to learn how to document the date, event/item, withdrawals, deposits, and keep a running balance.
Host a family game night.	Skills will vary based on the game, but may include: Strategy Basic facts Making change Spatial awareness		Designate one evening each week as "family game night" and enjoy some of the following math games: Q-bitz, Bop It!, Monopoly, Qwirkle, Blokus, and Rummikub.
Download math apps and games.	Basic facts Algebra Geometry Mental math Flexible thinking Spatial awareness Reasoning Logic Strategy		Check out Google Play or the iTunes store for ideas. Some popular games include: 2048, Nozuku, TanZen, and Lumos Learning's StepUp App.

Ask your child to choose just three of the activities on the list to start with. Try to start the first activity as soon as possible – today, if time permits! – and then work the other activities into your daily routine as you see fit. By asking for your child's input, you'll have a better chance of him or her "buying into" the idea of reviewing math concepts during the summer months. With games, apps, and time with family built into these suggestions, though, you shouldn't have much difficulty convincing your child that math can actually be a lot of fun!

SUMMER IS HERE! KEEP YOUR CHILD'S WRITING SKILLS SHARP WITH ONLINE GAMES

Like Reading and math, free online activities exist for all subjects… and writing is no exception. Check out the following free interactive writing activities, puzzles, quizzes and games that reinforce writing skills and encourage creativity:

Primary Level (K-2nd Grade)

Story Writing Game

In this game, the child fills in the blanks of a short story. The challenge is for the storyteller to choose words that fit the kind of story that has been selected. For example, if the child chooses to tell a ghost story, then he or she must select words for each blank that would be appropriate for a scary tale. http://www.funenglishgames.com/writinggames/story.html

Opinions Quiz for Critical Thinking

Practice developing logical reasons to support a thesis with this interactive activity. Students read the stated opinion, such as, "We should have longer recess because…" The child must then select all of the possible reasons from a list that would support the given statement. The challenge lies

with the fact that each statement may have more than one possible answer, and to receive credit, the student must select all correct responses. This game is best suited for older primary students. http://www.netrover.com/~kingskid/Opinion/opinion.html

Interactives: Sequence

Allow your child to practice ordering events with this interactive version of the fairy tale, Cinderella. The child looks at several pictures from the story and must drag them to the bottom of the screen to put the events in chronological order. When the player mouses over each scene from the story, a sentence describing the image appears and is read aloud to the student. Once the events are in order, the student can learn more about plot and other story elements with the accompanying tutorials and lessons. http://www.learner.org/interactives/story/sequence.html

BEATING THE BRAIN DRAIN THROUGH LITERACY: WEBINAR RECAP WITH PRINTABLE ACTIVITY SHEET

Lumos Learning conducted webinar on "Beating the Brain Drain Through Literacy." During this webinar, we provided the students with several ideas for keeping their literacy skills sharp in the summertime.

Here's a handy chart with the ideas from the webinar, ready for you to post on your refrigerator. Let your child pick and choose the activities that appeal to him or her. Of course, reading should be nonnegotiable, but the list below provides alternatives for reluctant readers – or for those who just don't enjoy reading a traditional fiction novel. The first set of activities touch upon ideas that reinforce writing skills, while the second half addresses reading skills. There is also room on the chart to date or check off activities your child has completed.

Skill Area	Activity	Completed this activity	Notes for parents
Writing skills, spelling, and/or vocabulary	Keep a journal (things you do, places you go, people you meet)		Even though journals work on spelling skills, be sure your child understands that spelling "doesn't count". Most children like to keep their journals private, so they don't need to worry about perfect skills or that someone else is going to read/grade what they wrote.
	Start a blog		Enable privacy settings to keep viewers limited to friends and family. Check out WordPress, Squarespace, and Quillpad to begin blogging.
	Get published		The following places publish student work: The Clairmont Review, CyberKids, Creative Kids Magazine, New Moon, and The Young Writer's Magazine.
	Write letters		Have your child write or type letters, postcards, and emails to friends and family members.
	Take part in a family movie night		Watch movies that are thought-provoking to elicit interesting post-movie discussions. Other good bets are movies that are based on a book (read the book first and compare the two).
	Organize a family game night		Choose word games to work on spelling and vocabulary skills (examples: Scrabble, Boggle, and Hangman).
Reading skills: fluency, comprehension, critical thinking, decoding skills,inferencing, etc.	Pick up a good book!		Places to find/buy/borrow books include: your public library, ebooks, yard sales, book stores, your child's school library (if it's open during the summer), and borrowed books from friends and family members.

	Read materials that aren't "books"…		Ideas include: karaoke lyrics, cereal boxes, newspapers, magazines for kids, billboards, close captioning, and audio books.
	Compete! Enter a reading challenge		Scholastic Reading hosts a competition called "Reading Under the Stars" to break a world record for minutes read. Barnes and Noble gives students the opportunity to earn one free book with "Imagination's Destination" reading challenge.

Note: Reading just six books over the summer can maintain – and sometimes even increase! – your child's reading level. Not sure if the book is appropriate for your child's reading level? Use the five-finger rule: have your son/daughter read a page of a book. Each time your child encounters a word that is unfamiliar or unknown, he or she holds up a finger. If your child holds up more than five fingers on a given page, that book is probably too difficult.

However, there are some books that a child will successfully tackle if it's high-interest to him or her. Keep in mind that reading levels are a guide (as is the five-finger rule), and some children may exceed expectations…so don't hold your child back if he or she really wants to read a particular book (even if it may appear to be too challenging).

Remember, if students do some of these simple activities, they can prevent the typical four to six weeks of learning loss due to the "summer slide." And since spelling, vocabulary and reading skills are vulnerable areas, be sure to encourage your child to maintain his or her current literacy level…it will go a long way come September!

WEBINAR "CLIFF NOTES" FOR BEATING SUMMER ACADEMIC LOSS: AN INFORMATIVE GUIDE TO PARENTS

The "Summer Slide"

First, it's important to understand the implications of "summer slide" – otherwise known as summer learning loss. Research has shown that some students who take standardized tests in the fall could have lost up to 4-6 weeks of learning each school year (when compared with test results from the previous spring). This means that teachers end up dedicating the first month of each new school year for reviewing material before they can move onto any new content and concepts.

The three areas that suffer most from summer learning loss are in the areas of vocabulary/reading, spelling, and math. In Stop! In the Name of Education: Prevent Summer Learning Loss With 7 Simple Steps, we discussed some activities parents could use with children to prevent summer slide. Let's add to that list with even more ways to keep children engaged and learning – all summer long.

Be sure to check out:

• Your Child's School

Talk to child's teacher, and tell him or her that you'd like to work on your child's academics over the summer. Most teachers will have many suggestions for you.

In addition to the classroom teacher as a resource, talk to the front office staff and guidance counselors. Reading lists and summer programs that are organized through the school district may be available for your family, and these staff members can usually point you in the right direction.

• Your Community

A quick Google search for "free activities for kids in (insert your town's name)" will yield results of possible educational experiences and opportunities in your area. Some towns offer "dollar days", park lunches, and local arts and entertainment.

You may even wish to involve your child in the research process to find fun, affordable memberships and discounts to use at area attractions. For New Jerseyans and Coloradans, check out www.funnewjersey.com and www.colorado.com for ideas.

Of course, don't forget your local library! In addition to books, you can borrow movies and audiobooks, check out the latest issue of your favorite magazine, and get free Internet access on the library's computers. Most libraries offer a plethora of other educational choices, too – from book clubs and author visits to movie nights and crafts classes, you're sure to find something at your local branch that your child will enjoy.

•Stores

This is an extremely engaging activity – and your child won't even know he or she is learning! For grocery shopping, ask your child to write the list while you dictate. At the store, your son/daughter can locate the items and keep a cost tally to stay within a specified budget. At the checkout, you can have a contest to see whose estimate of the final bill is most accurate – and then reward the winner!

You may wish to plan a home improvement project or plant a garden: for this, your child can make the list, research the necessary materials, and then plan and execute the project after a visit to your local home improvement store. All of these activities involve those three critical areas of spelling, vocabulary/reading, and math.

•The Kitchen

This is one of the best places to try new things – by researching new foods, recipes, and discussing healthy food choices – while practicing math skills (such as measuring ingredients, doubling recipes, etc.). Your child may also enjoy reading about new cultures and ethnicities and then trying out some new menu items from those cultures.

•The Television

TV doesn't have to be mind numbing … when used appropriately. You can watch sports with your child to review stats and make predictions; watch documentaries; or tune into the History Channel, Discovery, National Geographic, HGTV, and more. Anything that teaches, helps your child discover new interests, and promotes learning new things together is fair game.

As an extension, you may decide to research whether or not the show portrays accurate information. And for those children who really get "into" a certain topic, you can enrich their learning by taking related trips to the museum, doing Internet research, and checking out books from the library that tie into the topic of interest.

•Movies

Movies can be educational, too, if you debrief with your child afterwards. Schedule a family movie night, and then discuss how realistic the movie was, what the messages were, etc.

For book-based movies (such as Judy Moody, Harry Potter, Percy Jackson, etc.), you could read the book together first, and then view the movie version. Comparing and contrasting the two is another terrific educational way to enjoy time together and work on your child's reasoning skills.

Note: www.imdb.com and www.commonsensemedia.org are great sites for movie recommendations and movie reviews for kids and families.

•Games

Playing games promotes taking turns, reading and math skills, and strategy development. Scour yard sales for affordable board games like Scrabble, Monopoly, Uno, Battleship, and Qwirkle.

Don't forget about non-board games, like those found on the Wii, Nintendo, Xbox, and other gaming consoles. You'll still want to choose wisely and limit your child's screen time, but these electronic versions of popular (and new) games mirror the way kids think … while focusing on reading and math skills. For more ideas, Google "education apps" for suggestions.

•Books, books, books!

Of course, nothing beats reading for maintaining skills. When you can connect your child with a book that is of interest to him or her, it can be fun for your child, build confidence, and improve fluency.

To help your child find a book that's "just right", use the five-finger rule: choose a page from a possible book and have your child read that page. Every time he or she encounters an unknown word, put up a finger. If your child exceeds five fingers (that is, five unknown words), that book is probably too challenging and he or she may wish to pass on it.

For reluctant readers, consider non-book reading options, like:magazines (such as Ranger Rick, American Girl, Discovery Kids, and Sports Illustrated for Kids), cereal boxes, billboards, current events, closed captioning, and karaoke. If you keep your eyes open, you'll find there are many natural reading opportunities that surround us every day.

Whatever you do, remember to keep it fun. Summer is a time for rest and rejuvenation, and learning doesn't always have to be scheduled. In fact, some of the most educational experiences are unplanned.

Visit lumoslearning.com/parents/summer-program for more information.

Valuable Learning Experiences: A Summer Activity Guide for Parents

Soon school will be out of session, leaving the summer free for adventure and relaxation. However, it's important to also use the summer for learning activities. Giving your son or daughter opportunities to keep learning can result in more maturity, self-growth, curiosity, and intelligence. Read on to learn some ways to make the most of this summer.

Read

Summer is the perfect time to get some extra reading accomplished. Youth can explore books about history, art, animals, and other interests, or they can read classic novels that have influenced people for decades. A lot of libraries have summer fun reading programs which give children, teens, and adults little weekly prizes for reading books. You can also offer a reward, like a $25 gift card, if your child reads a certain amount of books.

Travel

"The World is a book and those who do not travel read only a page." This quote by Saint Augustine illustrates why travel is so important for a student (and even you!). Travel opens our eyes to new cultures, experiences, and challenges. When you travel, you see commonalities and differences between cultures.

Professor Adam Galinsky of Columbia Business School, who has researched travel benefits, said in a Quartz article that travel can help a child develop compassion and empathy: "Engaging with another culture helps kids recognize that their own egocentric way of looking at the world is not the only way of being in the world."

If the student in your life constantly complains about not having the newest iPhone, how would they feel seeing a child in a third-world country with few possessions? If you child is disrespectful and self-centered, what would they learn going to Japan and seeing a culture that promotes respect and otherness instead of self-centeredness?

If you can't afford to travel to another country, start a family travel fund everyone can contribute to and in the meantime, travel somewhere new locally! Many people stay in the area they live instead of exploring. Research attractions in your state and nearby states to plan a short road trip to fun and educational places!

Visit Museums

You can always take your children to visit museums. Spending some quality time at a museum can enhance curiosity because children can learn new things, explore their interests, or see exhibits expanding upon school subjects they recently studied. Many museums have seasonal exhibits, so research special exhibits nearby. For example, "Titanic: The Artifact Exhibition" has been making its way to various museums in the United States. It contains items recovered from the Titanic as well as interactive activities and displays explaining the doomed ship's history and tragic demise. This year, the exhibit is visiting Las Vegas, Orlando, and Waco.

Work

A final learning suggestion for the summer is for students to get a job, internship, or volunteer position. Such jobs can help with exploring career options. For example, if your child is thinking of becoming a vet, they could walk dogs for neighbors, or if your child wants to start their own business, summer is the perfect time to make and sell products.

Not only will a job or volunteer work look good on college applications, but it will also teach your children valuable life lessons that can result in more maturity and responsibility. You could enhance the experience by teaching them accounting and illustrating real world problems to them, like budgeting money for savings and bills.

The above suggestions are just four of the many ways you can help learning continue for your child or children all summer long. Experience and seeing things first-hand are some of the most important ways that students can learn, so we hope you find the above suggestions helpful in designing a fun, educational, and rewarding summer that will have benefits in and out of the classroom.

Additional Information

What if I buy more than one Lumos Study Program?

Step 1

Visit the URL and login to your account.
http://www.lumoslearning.com

Step 2

Click on 'My tedBooks' under the "Account" tab.
Place the Book Access Code and submit.

Step 3

To add the new book for a registered student, choose the
 button and select the student and submit.

To add the new book for a new student, choose the ⊙ Add New student
button and complete the student registration.

Lumos StepUp® Mobile App FAQ For Students

What is the Lumos StepUp® App?

It is a FREE application you can download onto your Android Smartphones, tablets, iPhones, and iPads.

What are the Benefits of the StepUp® App?

This mobile application gives convenient access to Practice Tests, Common Core State Standards, Online Workbooks, and learning resources through your Smartphone and tablet computers.

- Eleven Technology enhanced question types in both MATH and ELA
- Sample questions for Arithmetic drills
- Standard specific sample questions
- Instant access to the Common Core State Standards
- Jokes and cartoons to make learning fun!

Do I Need the StepUp® App to Access Online Workbooks?

No, you can access Lumos StepUp® Online Workbooks through a personal computer. The StepUp® app simply enhances your learning experience and allows you to conveniently access StepUp® Online Workbooks and additional resources through your smart phone or tablet.

How can I Download the App?

Visit **lumoslearning.com/a/stepup-app** using your Smartphone or tablet and follow the instructions to download the app.

**QR Code
for Smartphone
Or Tablet Users**

Lumos StepUp® Mobile App FAQ For Parents and Teachers

What is the Lumos StepUp® App?

It is a free app that teachers can use to easily access real-time student activity information as well as assign learning resources to students. Parents can also use it to easily access school-related information such as homework assigned by teachers and PTA meetings. It can be downloaded onto smart phones and tablets from popular App Stores.

What are the Benefits of the Lumos StepUp® App?

It provides convenient access to

- Standards aligned learning resources for your students
- An easy to use Dashboard
- Student progress reports
- Active and inactive students in your classroom
- Professional development information
- Educational Blogs

How can I Download the App?

Visit **lumoslearning.com/a/stepup-app** using your Smartphone or tablet and follow the instructions to download the app.

QR Code
for Smartphone
Or Tablet Users

Lumos tedBooks for State Assessments Practice

Lumos tedBook for standardized test practice provides necessary grade-specific state assessment practice and skills mastery. Each tedBook includes hundreds of standards-aligned practice questions and online summative assessments that mirror actual state tests.

The workbook provides students access to thousands of valuable learning resources such as worksheets, videos, apps, books, and much more.

Lumos Learning tedBooks for State Assessment	
SBAC Math & ELA Practice Book	CA, CT, DE, HI, ID, ME, MI, MN, NV, ND, OR, WA, WI
NJSLA Math & ELA Practice Book	NJ
ACT Aspire Math & ELA Practice Book	AL, AR
IAR Math & ELA Practice Book	IL
FSA Math & ELA Practice Book	FL
PARCC Math & ELA Practice Book	DC, NM
GMAS Math & ELA Practice Book	GA
NYST Math & ELA Practice Book	NY
ILEARN Math & ELA Practice Book	IN
LEAP Math & ELA Practice Book	LA
MAP Math & ELA Practice Book	MO
MAAP Math & ELA Practice Book	MS
AZM2 Math & ELA Practice Book	AZ
MCAP Math & ELA Practice Book	MD
OST Math & ELA Practice Book	OH
MCAS Math & ELA Practice Book	MA
CMAS Math & ELA Practice Book	CO
TN Ready Math & ELA Practice Book	TN

Available

- At Leading book stores
- www.lumoslearning.com/a/lumostedbooks